NICHOLAS THE CAT

CELEBRATES

NICHOLAS THE CAT CELEBRATES

By

ROBERTA BELANGER

FORWARD

Have you ever owned a cat? Or a dog? Dogs can do many things—chase a ball, go for walks. But what can a cat do? Sometimes they are very independent and don't want to play. Other times they want to help you with your homework and play with your computer.

Here are some stories and adventures about a cat who can do a lot! Nicholas the cat actually has a job. What? A cat with a job? He gets involved with dogs, other cats, even helps rescue horses. Nicholas trains to be a therapy cat. He has to wear a harness and leash just like a dog in order to visit patients in the hospital. A leash and harness? Piece of cake for Nicholas.

The Nicholas the Cat stories are a great gift for early readers. They will keep children curious as they enjoy his adventures. Hey Grandma, little ones love to listen to Nicolas's adventures, too!

NICHOLAS THE CAT SERIES

Nicholas the Cat
SAVES THE DAY

Nicholas the Cat
LENDS A PAW

Nicholas the Cat
CELEBRATES

Text Copyright ©2022 Roberta Belanger
Cover Illustrations Coyright©2022 Jeffrey O. McFarland
Nicholasthecat.com
Rbelanger1@verizon.net
All rights reserved. No part of this book may be used or reproduced in any manner whatsoever without written permission except in the case of brief quotations embedded in critical articles and reviews.
978-1-7346909-7-2

DEDICATION

Cherish your pets forever.

Nicholas
Smokey
Mocha
Phantom
Moose

TABLE OF CONTENTS

Family History
New Tour Boat in Town
Fog
Hannah Has a Tummy Ache
Therapy Training
Hospital Visiting Day
Magic, Mischief and Cypress
A Day of Surprises
Fireboat
Clambake
Toby
Blue Lobster
Rainy Day
Old Ironsides
Sunny Day
The Farm
Kindergarten
Hurricane
Beautiful Sunrise
Alex in Polynesia
Farewells

NICHOLAS'S FAMILY HISTORY

The small fishing village where Nicholas the cat lived with his Mom and sister is an old historic village. "Historic" means the village had been established and started hundreds of years ago. First one family settled in that area, more families came, and then many more.

The American Indians lived in the area first, and some of Nicholas's ancestors lived with them. It was a time for families, growing food, raising animals, hunting, and fishing. Life was harder in those days. There were no cars or trucks.

There were no grocery stores so families had to grow their own food. Video games? I don't think so! The American Indians built fires for warmth and cooking. They made their own clothes and they were expert hunters. Nicholas's Mom said, "I'm going to tell you about your great-great-great Aunt Elizabeth. She used to help the Indians with their fishing. The American Indians

fished from the canoes they had built, and she would go out fishing with them. She was not afraid of being out on the water and getting wet--unlike you, Nicholas!

"When the Indians went fishing and made a catch, they let the fish flip and flop in the bottom of their canoes. It was great-great-great Aunt Elizabeth's job to keep the fish from flipping back over the side and back into the water. Aunt Elizabeth would not let the fish escape. It was her job.

"Aunt Elizabeth was black and white, the same as me," Nicholas's Mom said. "She also had a white spot on the tip of her tail the same as your sister. The Indians decided the white spot on Aunt Elizabeth's tail brought good luck, and they were happy to have her help with their fishing." They respected and *celebrated* Aunt Elizabeth for all her help.

"People continued to come from Europe to settle in Nicholas's village. As different trading ships came into the harbor, the village grew and grew with more people, farms and houses. The big fishing dock has always been used for business. There was a time when ship building was done on the dock and it offered many jobs for the villagers. The original settlers were gifted ship builders. Ships were needed to bring supplies from the old country to Nicholas's village. The ships brought goods the settlers needed.

"There were many forests around Nicholas's village and the woodsmen cut the trees and shipped the lumber to other towns so they could build their houses and factories. Logging was big business.

"Whaling was also a big industry at that time. The captains of the whaling ships built beautiful houses along the harbor for their families. Many of them are still there. Roads were made of dirt and not paved as they are today. The villagers would tie the reins of their horses to hitching posts in front of their homes. The hitching posts were stone posts dug into the ground with a metal ring on the top so their horses' reins could be tied to it. Many of these hitching posts still stand today."

Speaking of stones, Nicholas had noticed how many stone walls there were in and around his village. New England is known for its stone walls, and especially around Nicholas's village. These rocks were piled into rows and walls to mark property lines. Imagine how hard the farmers and their helpers had to work to get the stones out of their fields so they could plow the land for their crops. What did they do with all the stones they took out of their fields? They built more stone walls! Rows and rows of them."

Nicholas's Mom said, "Inside the sea captains' homes there were many unusual and beautiful pieces of furniture and glassware that the sea captains brought back from their travels around the world. Captain Jeremiah Fowler was a famous seaman. His home overlooked the harbor and was on a beautiful, pleasant street. It was a short walk to the big fishing dock.

"When Captain Fowler was home from his whaling trips, he enjoyed playing with his children and his favorite cat. He had discovered a stray cat, or rather, the stray cat had discovered him as he stowed away on the captain's whaling ship during the last voyage." Nicholas learned that although this cat was a stowaway, he was welcome. As a stowaway, the cat didn't pay to get on board the ship. He was not hired to be a crew member. The cat snuck on board the boat one day as it was tied to the dock. This cat was all gray and white with a white tip at the end of his tail. He walked right up the gangplank. He saw lots of men getting on board the ship and decided he'd join them.

Nicholas's Mom continued, "He soon proved he was a good 'mouser.' That is important on a sailing ship. You don't want mice burrowing into the stored barrels of food on a long voyage.

"While on board, the cat followed Captain Fowler all over the ship. He seemed to know the Captain was an important person. The cat finally ended up sleeping in the Captain's bunk at night.

"Each time he caught a mouse, he delivered it to the Captain. The crew watched this stray cat rushing across the deck to bring his catch to the Captain. He would drop the mouse right at the Captain's feet, and would sit there looking up at him. The cat was not to be ignored. He waited for the Captain to thank him for catching the unwanted mouse.

"The whole crew would burst out laughing each time the cat performed his mouse trick. The cat had proven his worth to the Captain. He was pleased with the cat's talent for catching mice and he decided to name him Jonah.

"When Captain Fowler's ship arrived in port, Jonah trotted after him and followed him into the big house. Once the children saw Jonah, it was settled. He became the family cat."

Nicholas's Mom continued to tell Nicholas many stories about their ancestors from the old times when they helped the Indians, the whalers, and the 'old timers.' That's what they called the original settlers to Nicholas's area.

Nicholas listened to each story his Mom told about his ancestors. She continued with a story about Uncle Peter. Nicholas snuggled up to his Mom to let her know he couldn't wait to hear more of their family stories.

"Uncle Peter was a huge cat," his Mom said. "His fur was orange and black with a white spot on the tip of his tail. He was a tabby cat. Uncle Peter's eyes were large and bright yellow. His paws were white and they looked like small boots. When Uncle Peter moved around the farm, he held his tail way up high. As he walked through the tall grass, all you could see was the white tip of his tail swinging back and forth.

"Uncle Peter's job was to look out for the animals in the farmyard. He loved his job. The chickens were his favorite. The chickens were fed grain in the morning. They liked to scratch around in the yard and kept busy all day. Uncle Peter knew where the chickens laid their eggs, and he would help the children find them. The best part of his day was when he could relax, lay on the porch, enjoy the sunshine, and watch 'his' chickens.

"Uncle Peter's greatest problem was dogs," his Mom said. Nicholas could imagine neighborhood dogs coming into Uncle Peter's yard to chase the chickens. Uncle Peter did not care for dogs, and he didn't allow any dogs in his farmyard.

"One day," his Mom said, "Uncle Peter was sitting on the porch when a large dog came bounding into the yard. He did not see Uncle Peter resting on the porch. The dog made a leap for a chicken and Uncle Peter made a leap for the dog. He landed on the dog's back and stuck out his sharp claws. The dog yelped and jumped with surprise. The chickens squawked and ran away. Uncle Peter held on as the dog tried to race away. What a ride! That dog never came into Uncle Peter's yard again. Uncle Peter had *saved the day!*" After all it was his job."

Nicholas learned that in times of trouble, Uncle Peter would put his head down and use his huge yellow eyes to glare at an intruder as he threatened to pounce. "If you saw him hunch up his back with his fur standing at attention, watch out! No one looked scarier than your Uncle Peter. No one challenged Uncle Peter!" his Mom said.

During those old times, the people in the village didn't have refrigerators, but they knew how to take care of their food. Nicholas's favorite food was fish. "Have you ever heard of salt cod," his Mother asked? "Salted fish, usually cod, was a favorite recipe. The fishermen brought the codfish in to the big fishing dock, just the same as they do today.

"In the fall," his Mom continued, "when the ocean waters were cool, the cod fish were plentiful. The villagers would catch them and put them in ceramic pots and cover them with salt. The salt would preserve the fish for the whole winter."

People today still use salted fish mixed with potatoes as a favorite old New England recipe. They are called codfish cakes and they look like pancakes. The villagers cooked them over the fire in cast iron skillets. Delicious—a little salty—but delicious! Nicholas's Mom said "Uncle Peter loved them."

"How things have changed. Now there are huge farm tractors, cars, trucks, trains, airplanes, grocery stores, televisions, movie theatres, restaurants, schools, computers—everything you could think of. If you have a question, you can look up the answer on the internet. Can you imagine what the American Indians would have thought of the internet?" Nicholas imagined.

Nicholas knew that today farm animals are very important. They are treated with respect and kept healthy and safe. Today one can ride a horse for fun and the horse doesn't have to pull a plow!

"Hmmm, I have a long family history," thought Nicholas. He could imagine Aunt Elizabeth helping the American Indians fish from their canoes. Nicholas wasn't sure he could have worked in a canoe.

Nicholas thought about his Uncle Peter helping on his family's big farm. Chickens, dogs, children--it must have been a busy, busy day for him. Thinking about Uncle Peter enjoying the sun on the porch was nice. "I'm sure I would have liked to do that," Nicholas imagined.

Nicholas imagined whaling ships tied to the big fishing dock. It must have been hard work for the boss cat working on the dock in those days. "Maybe that's where Jonah worked when he wasn't out in Captain Fowler's whaling ship," Nicholas wondered.

Once in a while Nicholas liked to go out in the Captain's boat—that is, on a calm, sunny day when there were no big waves to toss him around. He imagined Jonah working out in the middle of the ocean on the whaling ships where the waves and storms could be fierce. There would be lightning and heavy rain. Water would drip from the rigging and the ship would roll from side to side in the rough seas. Waves would break and wash over the sides of the ship knocking the sailors down if they were not holding on. Many whaling ships were lost at sea due to the horrific storms.

"Where did Jonah hide when the big storms rolled in? Where did Jonah hide when sailors caught a whale and brought it on board? Not for me," thought Nicholas.

Nicholas felt proud that his relatives had had such exciting lives and were so helpful to their families. He could certainly *celebrate* his family's history. Now he would try harder and harder to help his Mom and sister, Misty, and do a good day's work each day on the big fishing dock. After all, that was his job.

NEW TOUR BOAT IN TOWN

Nicholas climbed down from his favorite tree this morning. The warm June air had helped him have a wonderful sleep. Last night before he went to bed, he noticed a beautiful red sunset. Colorful sunsets reminded him of an old adage his mother had taught him:

Red Sky in the Morning – Sailor's Take Warning!
Red Sky at Night – Sailor's Delight.

After last night's beautiful red sunset, Nicholas knew today would be a good fishing day for the men on the big fishing dock. Now it was time to check in and start his morning chores, but this morning soon turned out to be different.

Nicholas noticed a lot of people arriving at the big fishing dock. This meant something special must be happening. *A little exploration was called for, and Nicholas was good at that.*

More and more people kept arriving. Nicholas noticed it right away. Tied up next to the Captain's boat was an unusual looking boat. The boat didn't look like any other fishing boat at the big fishing dock.

The boat was long and not as wide as the Captain's boat. There was a small pilot house in the bow. There was a canvas roof that stretched from the pilot house all the way back to the stern of the boat. There were benches inside where people could sit. There was a sign on the top of the cabin that in big letters said "Tours."

There was a young man greeting people as they approached the boat. He was collecting tickets before he let the people get on board. "What is going on?" wondered Nicholas.

His friend Hap, a terrific lobsterman and special friend, came by and gave a whistle of appreciation. He liked the new boat and told Nicholas that this boat was going to be fun to have at the dock. Hap wore his usual bib-type overalls, a red t-shirt, and his cap on backwards. His pipe was stuck in between his teeth as always, but Nicholas knew he never lit it. He liked to chew on it for some reason. Curious!

As the morning moved on, Hap explained to Nicholas that the new boat was a tour boat. For a fee, it would take passengers on a guided tour to see seals and visit lighthouses.

In June, seals arrive in the harbors of New England. The cold waters and ice in the north drives them to Nicholas's harbor where the water is warmer. Seals can swim as far as 5,000 miles to get to the New England waters.

Seals are fast swimmers and can dive and stay underwater for as long as twenty minutes. Their favorite pastime is sunning themselves on rocks near the shore.

As the young man greeted the tour boat guests, he was watching Nicholas. He could tell that this cat was curious as Nicholas walked back and forth inspecting this strange looking boat. The young man began talking to Nicholas who had started to rub against the boy's legs. The tour guide scratched Nicholas's ears which, of course, Nicholas always enjoyed.

As the boat was about to start the tour, the young man invited Nicholas to come along. Nicholas couldn't resist. He jumped aboard. The Captain of the tour boat saw the cat jump into the tour boat. He asked the young man, "Why do we have a cat on board today, Ned?" Ned introduced Nicholas to Captain Jack. Captain Jack had sun-bleached blue eyes, weathered cheeks and a yellowing beard.

Captain Jack knew that Ned was fond of cats. The minute Nicholas jumped on board, all the guests wanted to play with him. Captain Jack could tell Nicholas was going to be a fun addition to his tour.

Nicholas jumped up on the control panel and sat next to Captain Jack. He tried to stay out of the way and not bother the guests.

As the tour got under way and headed out into the harbor, Nicholas could tell that Ned was the official tour guide. He explained to the guests, "Today we are traveling to see some harbor seals and gray seals with dark, dark eyes. Each seal can weigh three to four hundred pounds. Captain Jack will drive the boat as close to the seals as possible without scaring them.

"Captain Jack knows a trick so all of you will get a good look at the seals and be able to take pictures. He will put the boat engine in idle so the propeller will stop turning. The boat will slowly drift in the water, and that's when the seals get curious and approach the boat. It is almost comical to see a seal's head pop up out of the water, peek at the boat, and then quickly pop back down. Before long, another seal will do the same thing. Pop, Pop, Pop. One after another!" The passengers were clicking their cameras as fast as they could."

Ned continued, "The seals are looking for food. Their favorite food is fish, especially striped bass and eels." When Nicholas heard the word "eel," he remembered the young boy who caught an eel on the fish market dock. The boy took it off the hook and threw it back into the sea. Unfortunately, the boy leaned out too far as he watched the eel dive down deep. The boy fell in! *All is well that ends well,* as the boy was a great swimmer.

Nicholas also remembered how the young boy splashed water all over him as he climbed back onto the dock with his squishy, squishy wet shoes!

Ned explained, "Some seals have swum thousands of miles to get to Nicholas's harbor, and they are also scattered over many other harbors throughout New England. There was a time when seals almost died out. The Marine Mammal Protection Act of 1972 protected the seals, and now they are plentiful again.

"When too many seals move into the harbor, they can create many problems, however. First, seals can eat twenty to thirty pounds of fish daily. They are eating the fish the fishermen need to catch for their living. Sometimes seals can steal fish right off your fishing pole hook! Seals also like to take over the beaches so the tourists cannot enjoy swimming. So, while we enjoy seeing the seals come back into the harbor in June, there can be problems."

Ned told the tour guests, "Every creature has enemies. The enemy of all seals are sharks! Sharks like to catch seals." He continued, "I know it's scary to think of sharks chasing these cute little seals, but that is part of nature. Yes, I can hear you thinking about seals luring sharks into swimming areas. The Harbor Master and marine specialists keep a close eye out for the sharks."

Captain Jack steered the boat to several special seal areas and then drove it over to see a famous lighthouse in the Bay. Ned told the guests, "This lighthouse was retired from service twenty years go. That means the Coast Guard doesn't need it to warn ships from coming too close to the rocks anymore.

"Tourists can now visit and climb up into the lighthouse. The only way to get to this lighthouse is by boat, and that's why this new tour boat is so popular! Not only do you get to watch the seals, you get to climb up a lighthouse."

Captain Jack approached the island's dock and Ned secured the lines. "Please be careful as you climb up the lighthouse tower. The view from the top is wonderful. You will see all the boats sailing by. Seagulls may swoop around the top of the lighthouse hoping you will throw them a treat."

Nicholas saw Ned racing towards the lighthouse and he took up the chase. The two of them raced up the stairs to the top. It was an easy race for Nicholas, but Ned was huffing and puffing a little. Ned picked up Nicholas so he could see the view. He saw the tour boat tied to the lighthouse dock down below. From way up in the top of the lighthouse, the tour boat looked small.

Ned told the guests, "You will see a huge Fresnel lens on the top of the tower. When the lighthouse was active, the lens would light up and shine miles out into the sea to warn the passing ships to stay away from the rocks. There was a foghorn, too. You didn't want to be too close to the foghorn when it went off. The foghorn could also be heard miles out into the sea!"

Nicholas was so impressed with Ned and all that he knew about seals and lighthouses. He was looking forward to seeing more of Ned on the big fishing dock.

Nicholas was thinking it had been quite a long day out on the water. He knew as soon as the tour boat got back to the dock, he had to check in with the fishermen. First he would check on his friend, the Captain, and his big fishing boat. Following that, it was off to see John, the shell fisherman, and Hap, the lobsterman.

The day had been sunny, not too warm, with calm seas. That was a good thing for Nicholas. Sometimes when he was out in the Captain's big fishing boat, the big waves would make the boat rock and roll. Nicholas would have to hold on or end up on his nose.

The tour was over and Captain Jack steered the tour boat back toward the big fishing dock. Ned stood next to Captain Jack and started to sing. Everyone was surprised. Ned had a wonderful, loud, full voice and he sang an old sea shanty. The guests applauded when he finished singing. Nicholas never moved the whole time Ned was singing. He was astounded!

Ned stood up and explained to the guests what sea shanties were all about. "A shanty is a work song or folk song.

The words and music sets up a rhythm or beat that workers and sailors follow so they all pull or push together at the same time. Shanties helped the sailors row together or helped railroad men shovel coal into the boilers of the old steam engines."

Ned said, "I am going to call each one of you here on the tour boat today a *landlubber.* I'm going to teach you how to sing a real sea shanty. I'll be the Shantyman, the lead singer, and you will be the crew." He taught them the words and in no time they were all singing.

Shantyman: Oh, blow the man down, blow the man down!
Crew: To me way-aye, blow the man down.
Shantyman: Oh, blow the man down, blow him right down!
Crew: Give me some time to blow the man down.

Shantyman: As I was a-walking down Paradise Street,
Crew: To me way-aye, blow the man down.
Shantyman: A pretty young damsel I chanced for to meet!
Crew: Give me some time to blow the man down.

The guests started clapping along with the song as they felt the rhythmic beat. They were smiling and cheering each other and especially Ned.

The tour boat arrived back at the big fishing dock and Ned tied up the lines and helped the guests climb back onto the big fishing dock. They were all smiles which was a good sign for future tours for Ned and Captain Jack.

Nicholas stayed with Ned as the passengers left the boat. He was hoping to spend more time with him. Having Ned on the big fishing dock this summer was going to be fun.

Sometimes it's funny (funny peculiar—not funny ha ha!) the way things work out. First, Nicholas's friend the Captain stopped by to welcome Captain Jack and Ned to the big fishing dock when they returned from the tour. Ned mentioned to the Captain that his goal was to study music and sea shanties, but he needed to raise some money to help pay for his education.

The Captain remembered that the Johnson family had adopted Nicholas's little sister and that Mr. Johnson worked at the local university. He told Ned that he would introduce him to Mr. Johnson and maybe he would know of some part time jobs Ned could do. The Captain *saved the day*, again!

Nicholas was back on his job at the big fishing dock and it was time to give a last checkup on the mice and pesky seagulls. Nicholas had had a wonderful day on the tour boat, but his job always came first. He didn't see any mice near the fish nets and all the seagulls were floating in the harbor, so it looked as though his work day was done.

Now he was headed for his favorite tree in the park to have a long catnap. Tomorrow he would be back on the big fishing dock. After all, that was his job.

FOG

The fog comes on little cat feet.
It sits looking over harbor and city
on silent haunches and then moves on.

--Carl Sandberg

When Nicholas woke up this morning, he was quite chilly. His favorite sleeping tree was covered with dew. The sun wasn't shining because clouds had covered it. They were low, thick clouds that were rolling across the dock—at least what Nicholas could see of the dock.

Nicholas knew what the problem was. Fog. When it rolled in thick like this as it often did on a summer morning, Nicholas could barely see over to the dock. Water was dripping from the branches of the trees. It wasn't that it was raining, it was the moisture from the fog.

Fog is created when the water temperature is colder than the air. Most of the fishermen wouldn't be working today because it is difficult to see through the fog. A boat cruising through thick fog could run aground, or worse, run into another boat.

When the fishermen were out on the water, fog could roll in quickly during the day, too. When they saw fog rolling in, the fishermen would head back to the dock while they could still see their way.

Seamen know that when it's foggy, the seas are calm. That's a good thing. There would be no heavy waves to bounce the boats around. Fog brought calm and quiet on the water, but it brought danger as well.

The Captain had radar on his boat. Radar meant that he could see the channel markers and could safely make his way back to the dock. Smaller boats didn't have radar. Sometimes the smaller boats would follow the Captain's boat back to the harbor because they knew with his radar he could sail a safe course.

Now in modern times, people have GPS (Global Positioning System), especially on their phones. It is magic!

But the problem for the fishermen using GPS is that although it shows them where they on the map, it doesn't show them where the channel markers, buoys, or other boats sailing in the area are located. One boat could cause an accident by running into another boat. Nicholas's friend Hap had a close call last season.

Hap had seen the fog rolling in. He pulled in the last of his lobster pots and headed for the big fishing dock. About that time, Hap could hear a boat with a big engine noise heading his way. The speeding boat sprang out of the fog. There was nothing Hap could do but hold on when he saw it coming.

The power boat swerved away in time to avoid crashing into Hap's boat, but his waves pushed hard against Hap's boat. Hap had to hold on tight and some of his lobster pots slid across the deck.

It was about as close to a collision as you could imagine. Hap's boat settled down and continued on his way. The power boat never slowed down. It raced away.

Hap knew that boats without radar should not be on the water when it's foggy, let alone driving so fast. The driver of that boat was lucky that he did not run into Hap's big, solid lobster boat.

Fog differs from ordinary clouds as it is close to the ground and it reduces visibility.

The fog was so thick this morning that when Nicholas strolled over to the Captain's boat, he could not see the lobstermen's boats on the other side of the dock.

With any luck, the fog would "burn off" (evaporate) before too long, and the fishermen could go back to work.

Nicholas had also seen pictures of fog in the mountain valleys where it collected because the air was cooler in the valleys. That wasn't quite the same as what happened on the sea.

Large tankers and military ships had to take extra care when fog came calling. The big ships had radar and AIS (Automatic Identification Systems), of course, but they also needed to keep an eye out for the smaller boats that didn't. The large ships blew their horns with a long blast every two minutes to warn nearby boats that they were approaching

Nicholas knew that the Captain and his big boat had to be careful if he was traveling in the shipping lanes.

Airplane pilots have special flight instruments to help them take off and land whenever fog or bad weather is in the area.

They are trained to take off and land in bad visibility. Fog certainly qualifies for that!

The Captain was always happy to teach boat safety to new fishermen. He and Nicholas would take them out in his big boat to give them an idea of how radar worked, and how to get back to the dock if the fog became so thick that you couldn't see the shore.

Nicholas had heard the 'old timers' talk about fog. They would say, "The fog was so thick, I couldn't see my hand in front of my face!" That's extra thick fog, Nicholas realized. Those 'old timers' knew everything.

Nicholas would be happier today when the fog went away. Things were dripping wet. Water dripped off the rigging in the Captain's boat and plopped onto Nicholas's head. Not funny. His fur was getting all wet and matted down. I think you know cats don't like being wet—no swimming, no rain drops, no fog, and no baths!

"Here come those seagulls," thought Nicholas. "They don't care if things around them are wet." Seagulls know that fog doesn't form too high up in the air. They can fly above it if they soar up fifty to one hundred feet high! On a foggy day, seagulls like to spend their day swimming in the harbor. Water rolls right off their backs—just like on ducks! The mice, however, feel more like Nicholas. They take their tiny bodies and find dry places where they can wait for the fog to go away.

Nicholas arrived at the Captain's boat and he let out such a loud "MEOW" that the Captain almost jumped. Nicholas certainly got the Captain's attention and he understood what the problem was. He brought Nicholas into the cabin of his boat. Nicholas shook the water from his fur and it sprayed all over the cabin. It wasn't quite as bad as when Mr. Smith's dog, Lassie, had his soapy bath. Lassie shook, and shook, and sprayed soapy water all over whoever was standing too close. Nicholas shook enough to make the Captain flinch!

Nicholas visited in the boat cabin for a while. The sun was finally coming out which meant the fog would melt away. He could hear the fishermen arriving at the dock. Now that the fog was disappearing, they could go to work. The 'old timers' would say that the fog had 'burned off.'

That also meant the mice would come out and would crawl over the fish nets drying on the dock looking for a snack that might have been caught in the net. Not good, because as they were pulling a dried piece of fish out of the net, they could tear a hole in it.

Nicholas decided, "Time to get back to work. No mice on my watch!" He did a quick look around the harbor to see if the seagulls were lurking. So far, they were not threatening to land on the boats. Nicholas was on the job!

HANNAH HAS A TUMMY ACHE

Nicholas finished the first round of his visits to the big fishing dock for the day. His next stop was to see his friend John, the shell fisherman. John had saved him a little bowl of chowder that he had made for his supper the night before. Nicholas knew that John was quite a chef and his chowder recipe was the best! "Ah, breakfast," thought Nicholas.

That purring noise started up in Nicholas's throat and traveled all the way to the tip of his tail. John could hear Nicholas purring as he finished eating the chowder. Nicholas rubbed against John's legs as a thank you. John knew his chowder was a hit with Nicholas.

The lobstermen had left the dock early this morning to check their pots for lobsters and to set out new pots. It often takes several days before each pot is pulled up and checked to see if there are any lobsters inside. Yesterday the lobstermen had filled more lobster pots with bait from those smelly barrels. "Yuck! Phew!" Nicholas just walked away.

The lobstermen placed their pots in different areas of the bay. They knew that lobsters crawled across the sea bottom. New England lobsters are much in demand in the summer when the tourists eat all the lobsters the lobstermen can catch. New England lobsters are shipped all over the world and served in famous restaurants.

As Nicholas passed the Captain's boat, he remembered that the Captain said he was going to take a few days off. "I'm going to take my family on a little vacation. I need you to keep an eye on my fish nets and my boat while I'm away," the Captain told Nicholas. Nicholas was so proud that he could help. After all, that was his job.

Sure enough, as Nicholas looked around the dock, he could see that the mice were active again. As he came near, the mice scurried away. Nicholas had to watch them every minute.

Who should appear but his little mouse friend, Tim. Tim the mouse promised Nicholas that he had warned his mice friends to find a new place to play and to stay away from the fish nets. Nicholas knew it was unusual for a cat to have a mouse for a friend.

Tim was a cute mouse with a pink nose, pink ears, shiny yellow eyes, and tiny, tiny feet. Those feet could move fast and Nicholas knew Tim could also swim extra fast when he needed to. Tim scurried away to catch up with his other mice friends. "Imagine that," thought Nicholas, "I have a mouse assistant on the job!" That was pretty exciting and unexpected.

Things on the dock were quiet, so Nicholas decided to go up the street to visit Hannah and her Mom and Dad. They had had a terrific picnic after the Veteran's Day parade yesterday. When Nicholas got to Hannah's house, he found out that she was in bed
with a tummy ache. Her Mom and Dad were worried and had called the doctor.

The doctor said, "Please bring Hannah to my office so I can check on her condition." They put Hannah in the car and drove to the doctor's office. The doctor and his nurses were waiting for her.

They took her temperature and did some tests. The nurses made sure she was comfortable and gave her warm things to drink. When the tests were completed, the doctor told Hannah's family that she would be fine by the next day. He gave her some medicine to make her tummy feel better. The doctor said,

"Please bring Hannah to my office at the hospital for a final checkup tomorrow."

When they got home from the doctor's office, Nicholas was waiting for them. They told him about Hannah's visit to the doctor's office. Nicholas let Hannah put him in her doll carriage. She was happy to be home and she told Nicholas how good the doctor and the nurses were to her. Her tummy ache was all better. Nicholas spent the rest of the day snuggled up to Hannah in her nice warm bed. He sometimes nudged her with his cool nose.

Feeling better, she now wanted to play with her special friend. Nicholas purred and purred and purred. You might think that his purring motor would get tired, but it never did! Nicholas *celebrated* the fact that Hannah was well again.

Time for Nicholas to make his way back to the big fishing dock. He needed to make his final checkup on the fishing boats for the day. After all, that was his job.

THERAPY TRAINING

After visiting Hannah yesterday, Nicholas remembered his therapy training sessions with the Captain. The Captain was one of his best and oldest friends, but therapy training was tough! The obedience part of the therapy training was hard!

The Captain knew Nicholas had many of the qualities that would make him a good therapy pet. He loved people, and he liked to be held and petted. Not all pets are comfortable with that.

Nicholas saw many fishermen at the dock each day and they each had their own way of greeting him. One lobsterman loved to hold him and tickle Nicholas's feet. (Can you imagine?) Nicholas loved it. Other fishermen scratched his ears or gave him a hug.

As part of his training, learning how to *sit* and *stay* took some time, but the Captain was patient. To help Nicholas learn to sit, the Captain held some cat treats over Nicholas's head. When he looked up to see the treat, he automatically sat down. That took care of the *sit* part of his training. "Piece of cake!" decided Nicholas.

The *stay* part was another matter. It was another requirement in the therapy training course. The Captain would say *stay*, but Nicholas wanted to go, Go, GO! He wanted to chase something that he saw moving out of the corner of his eye. He wanted to find out what it was. Where did it go? Was it a mouse? Nicholas was great at exploring *and he was good at that*! But, no! He had to stay in one place until the Captain called him. This took time because Nicholas was one curious cat.

Also part of the training was learning to be comfortable wearing a harness with a leash attached. Nicholas had seen lots of dogs on a leash so he was sure if they could do it, he could do it, too. The first time the Captain buckled the harness on, it felt funny on his body. The harness was not too heavy, but it rubbed against his fur as he moved around. He gave his body a good shake to get the harness settled. The shake started at his head, traveled down his back and ended up at the end of his tail. It was a good one!

When the Captain added the leash to go with the harness, it was another matter! Cats are independent. Cats don't like to be told what to do. Cats go their own way at all times—except when they are on a leash. A leash is required for all therapy pets visiting patients, so Nicholas allowed the leash to be attached to his harness.

"What do you mean I can't go charging off by myself whenever I want to! What do you mean I have to stay right by your side! I don't want to go that way. I want to go this way!" exclaimed Nicholas. There was some interesting meowing that went along with this part of the training. Some loud. Some louder!

The Captain never jerked the leash but gently encouraged Nicholas to walk along beside him. There was always a treat at the end of their walk. Yes! "This might work," thought Nicholas.

HOSPITAL VISITING DAY

Today Nicholas woke up with a feeling of excitement. We all know he is very busy and needed to work on the big fishing dock. His job was to keep the seagulls away from having their lunch on the boats. What a mess they could make. They never cleaned up after themselves! They left half eaten fish and chewed up crabs all over the boat decks. Yuck! Not good. He had to admit that they were good at keeping the beaches clean, but they had this bad habit of using the boats as their dining room table. Not!

But why was Nicholas excited today? Because after completing his therapy cat training and practicing with the Captain on how to behave, it was time to pass the special test.

A nurse from the hospital had phoned the Captain. She asked the Captain to bring Nicholas to visit the children's ward. Today was the day!

As a therapy cat, Nicholas would have to travel by car to get to the hospital, nursing home, school or hospice center to visit the patients. That was all right with him. He liked riding in the Captain's big red truck. His cat carrier was comfortable and the Captain always put a soft towel or blanket in it.

The Captain put Nicholas's harness on him and attached the leash. Nicholas wasn't comfortable yet with the harness rubbing against his fur, but after giving his whole body a good shake, he got used to it.

The Captain had introduced Nicholas to the nurses some time ago. Nicholas proved that he could be quiet as he visited the patients and let them pet him. The nurses told Nicholas, "When you are sick and alone in the hospital, it is a wonderful treat to have an animal friend visit you."

The Captain put Nicholas in his cat carrier and drove him to the hospital. Nurse Patti met them at the hospital and took over. She gave Nicholas a nice hug and scratched his ears. "Today, Nicholas, we are going to visit many children." She took him to a room where a young boy was resting. She placed Nicholas at the

end of the bed. Nicholas sat still for a moment. As the boy saw Nicholas, his eyes got bigger and bigger and so did his smile.

Nicholas pretended that he was stalking his prey and crept up the bed. He was moving in slow motion. When he finally got up next to the boy, he pounced on him. The little boy was surprised and delighted. Nicholas let him hold him. He held still and was quiet. At this point Nicholas was purring and purring, and the boy was giggling. That reminded Nicholas of his special friend Hannah who was well known for her giggling.

Soon the boy fell asleep holding Nicholas and Nurse Patti gently picked Nicholas up and took him to another room.

Nicholas especially liked visiting the children's ward where there were four special beds. He made the children smile when he curled up next to them with his purring motor in high gear. He would hide under their blankets and pop up and gently pounce on them. That was a delight for the kids.

He would let them give him a ride in their wheel chairs. One wheel chair ride was so fast, Nicholas was afraid he might fall out!

One little boy had broken his leg. It was healing well. The boy used crutches and held Nicholas's leash with confidence as they went for a walk together.

The next room had two beds. The children couldn't wait to get their hands on Nicholas. "This is great," thought Nicholas. He and the children were having a great visit.

The purring never slowed down.

Nurse Patti was pleased with the way Nicholas acted with the patients. He was calm, happy to be petted and his purr was as loud as a lawn mower!

Nicholas also visited nursing homes and senior centers. Some of the homes did not allow the residents to keep their own pets, so when Nicholas visited, it reminded them of the wonderful pets they used to have at their homes. When Nicholas visited, they again had a pet to play with.

One of the senior residents said Nicholas looked almost the same as her old cat. She knew how to scratch his ears the right way. Of course, getting petted and hugged was what Nicholas liked the most.

Being a therapy cat made Nicholas feel happy. When he got home, he would tell his Mom about some of the patients he had visited. There was no doubt that Nicholas had proven that he was a good therapy cat. He had passed the test! He and Nurse Patti both looked forward to his next visit.

After the therapy visits, Nicholas headed back to the big fishing dock to check on those pesky mice and seagulls. After all, that was his job.

Nicholas **celebrated** his new job as a therapy cat.

He was *good at that*, too.

Who knew!

Grandma loves Nicholas

MAGIC, MISCHIEF and CYPRESS

MAGIC AND MISCHIEF

Hannah's Dad was enjoying his new job at the Santana Center. He loved living in the small New England fishing village with all the boats and old shops, but after growing up with horses on the family's ranch in Wyoming, Jim was happy to be working with horses again.

The Santana Center is a horse rescue center. Horses that had been abandoned for many different reasons were rescued, retrained, healed if they were sick or injured, and adopted by a new, loving family. Hannah's Dad found this job to be rewarding and he admired the owner, Kathy, for being so dedicated to this work.

Two new young horses had arrived. They were hackney horses and they were scared and skittish. Kathy couldn't get a halter on them. The two horses stuck together as if they were glued. If one moved, the other followed. If one went into the stall, the other followed. When one took a drink of water, the other one did, too. This went on day after day when they first arrived at the farm.

Kathy knew that that was all right. New arrivals to the farm needed to get used to their new home and surroundings.

Hackney horses are beautiful high stepping horses. Their front legs reached up high with sharply bent knees. They are famous for towing carriages and can trot at fast speeds.

Now that Hannah was in kindergarten and Nicholas could only play with her after school, he often visited the farm with her Dad Jim instead. Of course, that was after Nicholas had done his morning job on the big fishing dock. Net-chewing mice and pesky seagulls were an everyday problem!

Something interesting occurred one day at the horse rescue center that surprised Kathy and Jim. When Nicholas visited the farm, he stopped to look at the two new hackney horses. One of the volunteers named Barbara had named them Magic and Mischief. They were much smaller than the stallions. They were only about 147 cm tall (about five feet).

Nicholas walked over to their fenced yard which is called a paddock. Magic and Mischief looked carefully at Nicholas. No one moved. Nicholas wasn't sure if he should go into the paddock because, although Magic and Mischief weren't as big as Kaito and Hot Shot, they were still a lot bigger than he was.

Nicholas let them know he could be trusted because he sat still without moving and just watched them. That let the horses know that he liked them and wasn't going to chase or scare them. The horses needed a little time to get used to Nicholas sitting outside their paddock. Before too long, the young horses wandered over to where Nicholas was sitting. They were curious. Nicholas was curious, too.

Magic stuck her nose through the fencing and sniffed at Nicholas. Nicholas sniffed right back. I think Nicholas was more used to being around horses than the hackney horses were used to being around a cat. After all, Nicholas had ridden on a horse once, although then he was tucked inside Jim's shirt as a surprise for his daughter Hannah.

Now it was Mischief's turn to check out Nicholas. She pawed the ground a little because she was nervous, but Nicholas continued to sit still and watch. She pawed the ground again and again, but Nicholas continued to sit still and watch.

To let the horses get more used to being around people, Nicholas watched Kathy, the owner and trainer, put a chair inside their paddock. She sat down with a book in her hands. Hmmm.

"What is this person doing in our paddock?" they wondered. As time went by, they got more curious and stopped being so nervous. They approached Kathy. She made no effort to touch them and continued to sit quietly and read. Actually, she was only pretending to read; she was watching these two new hackney horses carefully!

Next thing she knew, Magic was nudging her book with her nose. Kathy remained quiet so she could see what would happen next. Mischief came along after Magic and nudged Kathy's knee. Kathy didn't move a muscle. The two horses wandered off for a while but soon returned to where Kathy sat.

This went on for about an hour and then Kathy got up, picked up the chair, and left the paddock. Of course, the minute she stood up, the two horses ran away but that was the beginning of their training.

The object was to get them used to being around people, getting them used to their new home, giving them plenty of hay and water, and always checking on their health. One step at a time.

After they had been at the Center for some months, Kathy began their training with a clicker. They took to it like fish to water. The clicker sound meant that there would be a reward for their doing a particular action or for behaving in a certain way.

The hackneys were ready to learn and they were extra smart. After careful training which took about six months, they accepted a saddle on their backs and could be ridden. Nicholas was impressed that these horses, who had been so scared when they first arrived at the Center, could now be ridden! "That's a huge success," he thought.

The most exciting thing was that Jim came home one day and told Hannah that Mischief and Magic had been adopted. Their new home would be in the State of Delaware where there were more hackneys. Mischief and Magic would be working with children at their new home. They were the right size for children—not too tall! A super happy ending. (Note: this is a true story!)

CYPRESS

Soon another special horse arrived at the Center. He seemed to be sad. His name was Cypress. Kathy wondered why someone had given such a beautiful horse the name of a tree! Maybe because Cypress trees stand so tall, and so did Cypress the horse!

All day long, Cypress pretty much stood in one spot in his paddock. Jim and Kathy had to encourage him to get him out of his stall. He hung his head down and didn't seem to be interested in what was going on around him. There were lots of other horses on the farm but he showed no interest in them. Every day Kathy or Jim would put a lead rope on him and walk him to the big paddock so he could get some exercise. Kathy could tell that Cypress had had good training. He knew how to walk, canter and trot on her command. But as soon as he got back to his stall, down went his head. Nicholas watched this routine on the days he went to the farm with Jim.

One day, Nicholas wandered into Cypress's stall and Cypress suddenly reacted. He picked up his head, reared up on his hind legs and started to run around. He was excited! Nicholas didn't understand what was happening. He headed for the exit fast. This horse was huge and Nicholas didn't want to get stepped on. But as soon as Nicholas left the paddock, the horse stopped and drooped his head down again and stood still.

Kathy watched this happen and she knew there must have been a relationship between Cypress and cats. Cypress reacted each time Nicholas came by. Kathy picked Nicholas up and carried him
into the paddock. She walked over to Cypress. She wanted to be sure Nicholas was safe but she also wanted the horse and cat to meet.

Cypress approached Kathy and was immediately interested in who she was carrying. He lifted his head and sniffed at Nicholas. Nicholas raised a paw and touched Cypress's nose. The horse liked that. Kathy put Nicholas down and Cypress started following
him around. Wherever Nicholas went, Cypress went. What a picture they made! This huge horse gently following a cat!

Kathy understood that wherever Cypress had come from, there must have been a pet cat that had been his friend and he was missing him. Bonds between different kinds of animals are sometimes unusual, but there can be a strong attachment.

Now, when Jim arrived at the farm, Cypress pranced over to the fence to see if Nicholas was with him. Sometimes Nicholas would sit on top of the fence post and Cypress would come over and nudge him. When Cypress went into the big paddock for his exercise, Nicholas would either lead him around or sit and watch.

Kathy was soon able to put a blanket on Cypress's back. She put Nicholas on the blanket and Cypress gave him a ride. You could tell by his gait that Cypress had never been happier.

Cypress continued his rehab training at the Center. Kathy soon determined that he was healthy, strong and ready to be

adopted. She let people know that he would make a wonderful horse for a
family. Sure enough, it wasn't long before a family with three teenagers adopted Cypress. Guess what! They had three cats at home. Cypress couldn't have been happier. He'd miss Nicholas, of course, but he was ready to start a new life with a new family—and three cats!

Nicholas would also miss Cypress. "How lucky I am to have a horse as a friend, especially one as large as Cypress," thought Nicholas.

Nicholas, of course, was also busy every day on the big fishing dock. The Captain had noticed his absence on the days he had gone to the Santana Center. He soon learned of Nicholas's adventure and friendship with a horse named Cypress. "Amazing," said the Captain. "Nicholas is one amazing cat!"

Nicholas had *saved the day—Again!*

A DAY OF SURPRISES

What was that wonderful smell? Something smelled like spring flowers and apple trees. The sharp senses in Nicholas's nose carried him out of the park and up the street. The aroma was getting stronger and it was coming from Hannah's house.

"That's it!" thought Nicholas. "Hannah's Mom must be baking again!" The last time she made an apple pie she served it with ice cream on the side. Nicholas remembered getting a bite—only of the ice cream, of course. But now when he smelled the apple pie baking, he remembered that ice cream. Baking apple pies meant ice cream!

That apple pie aroma pulled Nicholas right into Hannah's yard. He looked around to see what was going on. Hannah was playing
with her doll as she sat in the shade of her doll house. Her Dad had built her a special doll house that was so big, she could almost sit inside.

Nicholas crept around the back of the doll house and pounced on her. She let out a shriek and started giggling. The whole village knew about Hannah's giggles. Once they started, they were hard to stop. She started rolling around in the grass grabbing at Nicholas. She caught him and gave him a big hug which Nicholas liked, but would allow for only so long.

Nicholas knew that Hannah's Mom was an expert baker. She had graduated from a culinary school in Boston. The neighbors knew where to go when they wanted freshly baked bread and all kinds of desserts. Baking had become a successful business for Hannah's Mom, Eva.

She didn't need to advertise her baking business because it didn't take long for the neighbors to pass the word around. Now people throughout the village could place an order for her wonderful sweet treats.

For Hannah, however, it meant that her Mom was a busy person, and it also meant that she didn't have so much time to spend with Hannah. Hannah's Dad was also starting a new job so he wasn't around much either. Hannah understood that her parents had to work. She was glad to have Nicholas to play with.

Hannah was looking forward to the fall when she could start kindergarten. There would be lots of new things to learn and lots of new friends to meet. Kindergarten was a wonderful thing for Hannah, but Nicholas soon understood that it meant that Hannah would be at school and he couldn't play with her. Jobs and school were fun, exciting, and important, but it did make for complications.

Both Hannah and Nicholas had times when they felt a little lonely, but Hannah had a wonderful Mom and Dad, school would be starting soon, and Nicholas had his job at the big fishing dock. What could be better than that?

Today Nicholas and Hannah had had a good playtime, but now it was time for Nicholas to get back to his job at the big fishing dock. The Captain's boat was back at the dock and his fish net was pulled up in the air to dry. Some seaweed was stuck in the netting and had to be removed. Some shells were also stuck and had to be taken out.

Nicholas jumped from the dock onto the deck of the Captain's boat and found a small fish that was stuck in the netting. He was having a great time swatting at it and making the little fish wiggle. The Captain saw what was happening and removed the fish from the net and threw it overboard. He knew it would grow up and swim for another day. Nicholas was a little sad to lose his "toy" fish but he understood. No one was around who could play with him today.

As he was walking across the big fishing dock to where the lobstermen were, a seagull flying overhead dropped a quahog that barely missed hitting Nicholas. It went "splat" right in front of him and splashed quahog juice all over. What a close call! The seagull flew down to get his food and squawked and screeched at Nicholas. "Wait a minute! Wait a minute!" Nicholas yelled. "I didn't do anything!" The gull grabbed the quahog, spreading his wings so wide that they flattened Nicholas right to the ground as he flew off.

"What is going on!" sputtered Nicholas. "I'm having a weird day!"

Lots of visitors came to the big fishing dock each day to learn about the fishing fleet and maybe to buy some fresh fish or lobsters. Some days they all had their pets with them—especially their dogs. Today was no exception.

The owners spent more time keeping their pets from getting into trouble with other dogs than they did enjoying the boats, the sunshine and the pretty harbor. Leashes were getting tangled up, and the dog owners were blaming one another. Nicholas sat down and enjoyed watching the chaos! "Glad I'm not a dog," realized Nicholas.

One visitor drove up with her cat. The cat's owner didn't realize there would be so many dogs on the fishing dock, and when she opened the car door to do some shopping, her lady cat escaped from the car. Nicholas spied the new arrival and knew right away that it was a beautiful Persian lady cat. Her fur was long, fluffy and gold in color. She was elegant and looked like royalty. She had a cute snub nose.

The dogs saw the Persian lady cat too, and the chase was on. The Persian headed for the end of the dock. Nicholas, in turn, was chasing after the pack of dogs as he was worried about the lady cat.

The Persian had to protect herself so she jumped into the Captain's boat and climbed the net that had been hung up to dry in the sun. Nicholas stopped and shook his head. He had never seen a cat climb that high that fast!

It all happened so fast that the Captain couldn't believe what he had seen. A cat climbing up his net with a pack of dogs howling at her from the dock. The pet owners were out of control, and there sat Nicholas, watching with a smile on his little face. What a fiasco!

The Captain shook his head. He suggested the dog owners control their dogs and leave. He lowered the net so the owner could retrieve her Persian. She was grateful to the Captain for the rescue. Yes, the Captain *had saved the day!*

The beautiful Persian cat sauntered over to Nicholas and they touched noses. That's a special greeting among happy cats. She told Nicholas that her name was Francine.

After their visit, Nicholas was sorry to see Francine leave his dock. The owner picked Francine up and carried her back to the car. The beautiful Persian turned her head to take one more glance at her new friend, Nicholas. Nicholas sighed. "I'd like to see her again."

As things quieted down, Nicholas continued his stroll over to the other side of the big fishing dock to check on his lobstermen friends. They were busy putting new bait into the lobster pots for tomorrow's work.

"Here we go again," thought Nicholas. "I started my day with the wonderful aroma of apple pie (which meant ice cream to Nicholas) and now smelly lobster bait! "Yuck. Phew! Think I'll come back another time."

Next he strolled over to visit John, the shell fisherman. John was happy to see Nicholas and asked him to watch his basket of quahogs. John had arrived back to the big fishing dock with today's catch, but he had had some engine trouble with his powerful outboard motor. He needed to run home and get some tools to fix it. He didn't want the seagulls to steal his quahogs while he was away.

Nicholas was on the job! He looked around and sure enough there were several seagulls stalking that basket of quahogs. They walked closer and closer. These seagulls were much bigger than Nicholas, but he was not afraid. He was the boss of the dock.

Nicholas bravely charged toward one gull and hissed at another one. The gulls rose up and flapped their huge wings and screeched but not enough to stop Nicholas. He leaped on top of the basket of quahogs and the seagulls knew that they had lost the fight. Nicholas had *saved the day!* Off they flew but Nicholas knew they would be back in a flash if he left the dock. Not today!

John returned soon with his tools and thanked Nicholas for the help. "Ah ha!" Nicholas's nose was working again. Now what was that aroma? The villagers knew that John was a wonderful chef, and while he was at his house, he had put some leftover baked fish on a little plate for Nicholas as a thank you. "Wow! I'm eating John's baked fish for lunch," Nicholas purred. Maybe that's why John was Nicholas's favorite shell fisherman.

Nicholas's work day was drawing to a close. Most of the fishermen were headed home. Nicholas did one more walk around the dock to check on what was going on. The mice were nowhere to be seen and the seagulls had had enough of Nicholas for one day. They were off swimming in the harbor.

Nicholas headed back to the park to visit his Mom and get ready for a nice snooze in his favorite tree. He was thinking that you never know at the start of the day how things will turn out at the end.

Let's see—giggling Hannah and her doll house, helping the Captain clean out his fish net, almost getting hit by a falling quahog, a fight between a group of dogs, meeting a beautiful Persian lady cat named Francine, lobstermen with their smelly bait, quahog-stealing seagulls at John's boat, and finally a delicious baked fish treat.

"Not bad for one day! And tomorrow I'll start all over again. After all, that's my job," sighed Nicholas.

FIRE BOAT

Nicholas work up after his good night's sleep in his favorite tree. He stuck out his front paws and took a long stretch. The tree in the little park had always been his favorite place to sleep. His favorite branch was up high enough so he could look out over the whole park to be sure everything was calm. He thought it was going to be a lovely, quiet morning. Nicholas had the park all to himself.

Nicholas was hoping, however, that his little sister Misty, might come by for a visit today. He knew she was so happy to be with her new adopted family, the Johnsons. Their twins were taking good care of her and played with her in the morning before they went to school. Sometimes Misty was happy to see them go, however, so she could get a little rest. When the twins tossed a tiny ball for her, she went after it like it was a soccer ball. If they threw a tiny catnip mouse in the air, she would leap up in the air, catch it, and run around the house with her prize.

One of the children's favorite games with Misty was to take a page out of the local newspaper and make a tent of it on the floor. Misty would hide underneath. As the twins scratched on the outside of the newspaper, Misty would attack. The twins would get into fits of laughing watching her play. When the twins went off to school, Misty was definitely ready for a catnap.

Nicholas was about to head over to the big fishing dock to start his work day, when he heard a lot of commotion coming from that direction. Cars were arriving one after the other. A fire truck with its sirens blasting drove onto the dock. "Oh, no!" Nicholas saw a television truck with its tall antennae aimed toward the sky. Newsmen and cameramen were heading over to where the Captain's big boat was docked.

What was happening? Nicholas couldn't get over there fast enough to find out what was going on. He was afraid there was a fire on the dock or a problem with the Captain's boat. Maybe the lobstermen were in trouble! He wound his way through all the legs on the dock while trying to figure out what was causing the excitement.

Then he saw it. A new boat was arriving at the big fishing dock. It was a fire boat from the town's fire department. "Wow!" The boat was almost forty feet long and it was painted a bright red. He heard one of the firemen say that the boat had an 860 horsepower jet blast engine. "A jet engine on a boat?" wondered Nicholas. He figured that meant it could go pretty fast, for sure.

The firemen operating this boat needed special training for the marine operations. Three fire fighters were needed to run the boat: a deck hand, a navigator, and a boat operator.

Nicholas heard one fire fighter tell the television newsman that the boat would be used to put out fires and for search and rescue missions on the water. The boat was owned by the Town in conjunction with the U. S. Coast Guard and the Bay Marine Task Force.

One of the worst things that could happen to sailors was to have their boat catch fire while they were at sea. "How would you put out a fire if you were on your boat all alone?" Nicholas wondered. Every boat is required to have a fire extinguisher on board, but that might not be enough. The good news was that now the boat owner could call the fire department or the Harbor Master or 911, and the new fire boat would come to the rescue.

The fire boat could spray foam a long distance to put out a boat fire and rescue the sailors. "Imagine that!" exclaimed Nicholas. "A fire department right on the water."

The Captain and other fishermen on the big fishing dock were interested in this new fire boat. All of them would be safer as they went to work on the water.

Nicholas remembered that lots of fire departments had those spotted dogs sitting on top of their fire trucks. "Let's see, I think they are called 'Dalmatians,'" thought Nicholas. "I hope the fire boat won't have one of those dogs hanging around my dock all the time. The shell fishermen all had dogs on their boats, and that was enough!"

Nicholas noticed a young boy sitting on a park bench with his Mom watching the new fire boat make its way to the dock. The boy seemed a little nervous as he swung his legs back and forth. His feet didn't reach to the ground. Nicholas strolled over to him and rubbed against his legs. The boy immediately reached down and picked Nicholas up. He bent over and buried his face in Nicholas's fur. Because Nicholas could sense that the boy was under a lot of stress, he let the boy hold him and he held very still.

The boy's mother was sitting next to her son and Nicholas heard her tell the television reporters that the boy had been on his Dad's boat last summer when the gas tank caught fire. His Dad had used the fire extinguisher he carried on the boat, but it wasn't enough to put out the fire. He realized it was best to abandon the boat and swim away from it.

The boat wasn't that important, but of course, his son was. What saved them was that the boy and his Dad always wore their life preservers when they were on the boat. Together, he and his son had jumped into the water and swam away from the fire.

A nearby boat saw the accident happen and immediately called the emergency call number. The call was transferred to the local Harbor Master and the fire department. The fire boat responded fast and raced over to where the boy and his father were in the water. They carefully brought the two onto their boat. No one was hurt but, needless to say, they were pretty shaken up. The boy's Dad sat with his son and never let go.

The Harbor Master also arrived to lend a hand. He towed the damaged boat back to the dock. The fire was out but there was a lot of damage. It was the rescue that was important.

Today as the young boy sat on the dock, he remembered the boat fire and how scared he had been until the fire boat arrived. The firemen had used the foam hoses to put out the fire.

A fireman on the new fireboat saw the young boy sitting on the bench holding Nicholas, and remembered the boy's boat catching fire that summer day. He invited the young boy to come aboard and see their new boat. The boy was curious. He was still holding Nicholas and wouldn't let go. He let the fireman lower him and Nicholas onto their new boat. The boat was shiny and new.

Nicholas started to purr as he could sense that the boy was pretty excited about getting the chance to get onto the new boat. He wasn't so scared any more. After the boat tour, the firemen returned the young boy and Nicholas to the dock.

The firemen took the fire boat out into the middle of the harbor and demonstrated the power of the foam hoses. The boy was jumping up and down with excitement. Nicholas, however, was getting a little tense. The boy gave Nicholas a final hug and put him down. "Whew!" The boy's mother bent down and scratched Nicholas's ears. She was saying thank you to Nicholas for letting the little boy use him as a safety outlet.

Nicholas knew that firemen were also sometimes called when a cat got a little too curious and climbed too high up into a tree. When the cat discovered it couldn't get down, there was a lot of meowing and its owner knew who to call—the local fire department! Why? Because they had the tall, tall ladders that could reach up to the cat. Nicholas wondered if the firemen had to have special training in order to rescue a cat!

"That was a pretty exciting way to start my morning," thought Nicholas. The fire boat was amazing and he was glad it would protect all his fishermen friends and all the local boaters. The fire trucks were leaving the big fishing dock, and the news trucks had lowered their antennae and driven away.

Finally, the dock was quiet. Nicholas liked it that way. Nicholas made his rounds to make sure the seagulls and mice were not bothering anything. After all, that was his job.

FOURTH OF JULY CLAMBAKE

In New England where Nicholas the cat lives, clambakes are famous, popular and the food is delicious. If you are invited to a clambake, you are in for a treat.

What is a clambake? It's a collection of seafood including fish, lobsters, clams and you can add some potatoes, sausage and chicken. There are lots of different foods you can put in a clambake, and there are lots of different ways to cook a clambake.

John, Nicholas's favorite shell fisherman, had a special recipe. All the villagers knew what a wonderful cook John was. Most of his friends called him "Chef John." His recipe called for steaming the clams, and that's why it's called a clambake. You'll never guess how he did it.

Summer had arrived which meant that the Fourth of July holiday was coming soon. The whole town had plans to *celebrate* at the Town Beach. The Town Band was always invited to play patriotic songs. People brought picnics and sat on the grass to hear the music. When it got dark, there were fireworks to watch.

Nicholas felt that the lights shooting up in the sky were pretty, but he didn't like the big "boom" at the end. He liked to watch the fireworks with his Mom and sister in the little park next to the big fishing dock. He was safe there from the loud noise. He knew the noise wouldn't hurt him, but it was extremely loud! It made his little sister jump!

This year, Nicholas's favorite shell fisherman, John, decided to have a clambake on his beach as a way to *celebrate* the Fourth of July. John could easily walk from his beach house to the big fishing dock where he worked.

Preparing a clambake takes a lot of work and John had many friends who were willing to help. The Captain said, "I'll catch all the fish you need for the clambake." Another friend supplied corn on the cob from his farm--a real summer treat. Nicholas had tasted corn on the cob and he liked it. It was tricky to bite the corn as it kept rolling away from him. "There he goes again," said John, as he and the Captain laughingly watched Nicholas chase the corn as it rolled across the kitchen floor.

John decided he would add sausages to his clambake this year. They were made by a local butcher in his shop. Lobsters, of course; you had to have lobsters. They are placed at the top of the bake.

Now for the secret ingredient to make a real New England clambake--"rock weed." John told Nicholas that "rock weed" is a seaweed that grows on the rocky shores of the ocean. Rock weed is green and has little bubbles in it. The bubbles are full of sea water.

Nicholas sniffed it and it did smell like sea water. He took a bite. "Oh, no!" The seaweed bubbles burst and sea water squirted out and sprayed his face. Not funny! He spit it out. *Nicholas liked exploring new things and he was good at it*, but it got him into trouble sometimes. He did not like getting wet! John would soon show Nicholas how important rock weed was in a clambake.

John invited many of his fishermen friends and their families to the clambake. John had planned a big Fourth of July party, but first there was work to be done.

He gathered piles of firewood. He also collected lots of rocks. "Rocks?" thought Nicholas. "You can't eat rocks." John began his clambake by building a bonfire made with all the wood and small logs from his beach. The wood pile grew tall and looked

like an Indian teepee. Inside the wood pile, he placed the rocks. John ignited the bonfire with the rocks inside. The bonfire got super, super hot. But why were rocks in the bonfire?

While the rocks were heating, the guests gathered around John's beach to enjoy clam chowder. People in New England like to put little round crackers on top of their clam chowder. They are called "oyster" crackers. Nicholas did not understand. "They don't look like oysters. They don't taste like oysters either," Nicholas realized. But the "old timers" liked oyster crackers in their clam chowder and there was no arguing with that.

John had prepared a special wooden barrel to hold all the clambake food. A barrel? The wooden barrel looked like the barrels the whalers had used on their ships. Next he buried the barrel in the sand. What? This was the first clambake Nicholas had been to and he was learning a lot, but putting the barrel down deep in the sand? He didn't think sand and food would mix well.

John called to his helpers, "The rocks are ready!" Some of the heated rocks were glowing red. Children and pets had to stay away! John and his fishermen friends picked the heated rocks up with shovels and carefully put them in the bottom of the barrel keeping them away from the sides of the wooden barrel so it would not burn. Next came the rock weed. This seaweed was wet with its little pockets of sea water and it sizzled as it hit the heated rocks. What next?

John placed all the food in special fishnet-type bags. The Captain made these bags the same as he made his giant fish nets. When the clambake was cooked, it was easy to pull these bags out of the barrel, and place them on the tables. The bags were cut open and the food was put on trays for serving.

John had dug lots of clams for the clambake right on his beach. After all, he was an excellent shell fisherman. He caught hard shelled quahogs and soft "steamer" clams. This created wonderful steam that would cook the food. The steam from the rock weed also added wonderful flavor to the bake as it cooked. Next came the bags of clams and the rest of the food. Lobsters, of course, were on the top of the barrel of food.

The last secret for a successful clambake was a huge potato. It was placed on the top of all the food. When the potato was cooked, the chef knew the whole clambake was ready to eat.

Clean canvas fabric was fastened over the top of the barrel. Sand was spread onto the edges of the canvas top. That would keep the steam from escaping. The steam was needed to cook the food and John knew that with good steam, the whole barrel of food would be ready to eat in about an hour. The aromas coming from the barrel were floating in the air. Delicious!

Rethinking all that he had learned about clambakes, Nicholas was astounded at John's knowledge. How did he learn how to make a New England clambake? There are many different ways you can cook a clambake, but John had learned how to do it from the "old timers" in his family and from his ancestors.

While the clambake was cooking, Nicholas saw a group of children playing baseball on the beach. Another group was kicking a soccer ball around. Some children were swimming. Sand was blowing all over the place! There was lots of laughter. Nicholas, of course, stayed away from the water!

Some of the Dads joined in the baseball game but they hit the balls so hard that they kept flying out into the deep water. When they ran out of baseballs, the children went back to playing soccer without the Dads.

There were also some dogs at the clambake, but they were friendly. Nicholas ran over to Mikey, the golden retriever therapy dog he had met in the hospital, and they shared and chased a ball. When it drifted into the water, Nicholas let Mikey go after it!

Hannah and her Mom and Dad came to the clambake, too. John was teaching Hannah's Mom how to cook seafood and she, being a baker, brought dessert.

Nicholas's Mom and sister were also invited. They let the little children pick them up and pet them. They sat on Hannah's blanket. His Mom and sister were purring happily.

The children made all kinds of sand castles. When the tide came in, they would be washed away. "That's all right," said Hannah's Mom. "You can always make more another day."

When the clambake was fully cooked, all the guests helped serve the delicious seafood. Now it was time for the fireworks! "After all," thought Nicholas, "it is the Fourth of July." Chef

John and his clambake had given all the guests a wonderful Fourth. They all had a good time. He and his fisherman friends ha
d *saved the day!*
What a special treat!
> What a **celebration!**
> A New England clambake is not to be missed.

TOBY AND THE KITTEN

Nicholas had finished his morning chores on the big fishing dock. Most of the fisherman had left the dock and motored out to their fishing grounds. The seagulls and net-chewing mice were under control, and Nicholas decided it would be a good time to head back to his favorite tree in the park next door for a little catnap. He climbed up to his favorite branch and was about to take a snooze when, to his surprise, the oddest thing Nicholas had ever seen came walking into his little park.

Nicholas saw a small dog walking into the park with a little kitten beside him. He thought the dog was full grown because he looked nice and solid. He body was long and he had short stubby legs so he walked close to the ground. His fur was a light brown and white. He had tall ears that stuck up from his long nose, but he had a gentle face with bright alert eyes. His face looked like he was smiling. He also didn't have a tail! What? Nicholas was sure all dogs had tails.

The dog continued to lead the kitten into the park. The kitten looked young and had a cute baby face. He was all black and his

fur looked a little fuzzy because he was so young. His short pointy tail stuck up in the air.

Nicholas wondered, "What was this dog and cat doing walking into the park by themselves? Where was their family?" He climbed down from his favorite branch and watched these new arrivals for a while.

Nicholas later found out that the dog was a Corgi. The Corgi herded the kitten over to the little fountain that had nice fresh water in it, and they both took a long drink. Next they laid down in the shade.

At this point, Nicholas's curiosity got the best of him. He approached the Corgi and kitten. He sat nearby watching them and didn't say anything. The Corgi, who appeared to be a little nervous, asked, "Who are you?" Nicholas told him, "My name is Nicholas. I live in this park and work on the big fishing dock next door. It's nice to see you in the park. Where do you come from?" And that's when the confusion started!

The Corgi and the kitten both started talking at the same time and although it was only a kitten, he "meowed" louder than the dog could speak.

The Corgi took over the conversation and told Nicholas that their family had been vacationing in Nicholas's village, but when they woke up this morning, the family was gone. The dog said he had heard the family van engine start up, but he didn't realize they were leaving. He and the kitten were left all alone.

They had no idea what to do. They waited inside the rented cottage one whole day, but decided they had better go out and see if they could find their family. They managed to open the screen door and get outside. No one was around. There was no trace of the family. They started walking and wandered into Nicholas's little park.

Nicholas could tell that these two strangers needed help. Nicholas said, "Stay here in the park for a few minutes. I have an idea." Nicholas raced over to the Captain's boat on the big fishing dock. The Captain was his best friend and he knew he could help, but the Captain had already left the dock and gone out fishing.

Nicholas looked around and saw John, his favorite shell fisherman, over on the other side of the dock. He was getting ready to leave in his boat. Nicholas raced over to John and caught him before he could start his engine. Nicholas made such a commotion of meowing and racing around in circles that John knew something was wrong. Nicholas was almost climbing John's leg!

Nicholas raced toward the neighboring park, then raced back to John. Loud meowing! Nicholas raced back toward the park again. Louder meowing! John finally got the message that Nicholas wanted him to follow him.

When John got to the park, Nicholas led him to the fountain area where the Corgi and kitten were resting.

John had never seen these pets in the neighborhood before and wondered where they came from. He wondered why their owners weren't with them. But first, he figured they might be hungry, so he went to his house nearby and brought back some kibbles for the Corgi and some tuna fish for the kitten.

Boy, were they hungry. They went after the food like they hadn't eaten in days and that, of course, was exactly what had happened.

John noticed that the Corgi was wearing a dog collar and the Corgi let John read the tags that were on it. The tag said the Corgi's name was Toby. Toby had come all the way from New York. John didn't think he could have walked that far on his little legs, so the best thing to do was to find the family.

He called Animal Control and read the information on the tag to the agent. The agent checked the tag information and found out that they belonged to the Fuller family in New York. That was a long way away!

The agent located an address and phone number that was on the Corgi's tag. When the agent called Mr. & Mrs. Fuller, they were so excited to hear about their pets. They had been frantic to find them.

The Fullers figured out what had happened. As they were packing up to leave the summer rental cottage, they had packed their van with all their vacation gear--chairs, umbrellas, the charcoal grill, beach towels, all their summer clothes, and everything else you could think of—plus their two children.

Mr. Fuller thought *his wife* was going to put Toby into his travel cage and put Midnight, their new kitten, into his carry case. Mrs. Fuller thought *her husband* was going to pack up their pets!

Uh, Oh! Neither one of them took care of their pets! How could this have happened?

Maybe it was because their two young children where keeping them pretty busy. No excuses! Never! The children were in tears!

It occurred to the Fullers that because it took less than three hours to drive from Nicholas's village to their New York home, they hadn't made any stops along the way. It wasn't until they reached their New York home and were unpacking their van, that they began to panic. Toby and Midnight were not in the van.

They called the landlord of the rental cottage in Nicholas's village, and he rushed right over to the house. He saw that the screen door was open, but the pets were not inside. Now what?

"All's well that ends well."

In the meantime, John brought Toby and Midnight, the kitten, to his home so they would be safe. The Animal Control agent let John know that Mr. Fuller would be driving back right away to pick up his pets.

When he arrived at John's home, Mr. Fuller was so happy to find that his pets were all right. Toby and Midnight jumped all over him. They were, obviously, glad to see him again. It was a real *celebration!*

John made sure to tell Mr. Fuller that Nicholas had *saved the day* when he directed John into the park. What a wonderful rescue. Nicholas was feeling quite proud of himself—and he deserved it! Mr. Fuller packed Toby and the kitten, Midnight, into his van. He was thinking how happy his children would be when he and his pets arrived back home.

Now back to work on the big fishing dock. Pesky mice and seagulls needed constant attention, and Nicholas was good at that.

After all, that was his job.

WHY SO BLUE, LOBSTER?

Before he was fully awake from his afternoon nap, Nicholas heard commotion coming from the big fishing dock. All the fishermen had gone out fishing this morning, so Nicholas had gone back to the park to take a catnap on his favorite branch on his favorite tree. But, the noise! Car after car and truck after truck were driving onto the big fishing dock. Nicholas was super curious about what was happening?

He jumped down from the tree and scurried over to the big fishing dock as fast as he could go. He was worried one of his fishermen friends had met with some kind of danger.

All the excitement was coming from the lobstermen's side of the dock. "Oh, No! I hope Hap is all right," worried Nicholas. Hap was his favorite lobsterman.

Nicholas saw his best friend the Captain and John, the shell fisherman, in the crowd, so he knew they were all right. Nicholas wound his way through the crowd of people that were gathering around Hap, his lobsterman friend. Hap had a big smile on his face. He wore his usual bib-type jeans with his red t-shirt and a cap that was always on backwards. So far so good.

Cameramen were arriving and a television van pulled onto the big fishing dock. There stood Hap on the deck of his lobster boat. He was holding up a blue lobster? A what? Lobsters aren't blue! They are green in the ocean and red when you cook them.

Blue? Nicholas soon got an education about why a lobster can be blue. The lobster shell produces more of a certain protein than normal, so it turns blue. You would almost have to be a scientist to know that!

There was so much excitement! Nicholas heard Hap tell everyone that the chances of catching a blue lobster was one in two million! They are rarely found in New England waters but one had walked right into Hap's lobster trap.

Blue lobsters feed on mollusks, fish and sea algae the same as other lobsters. They are the same as all American or European lobsters—except for the color, of course.

Did you know that all lobsters have a good sense of smell and taste, but blue lobsters have poor vision. "Maybe that's why it walked into Hap's lobster trap," decided Nicholas. "Hap would tell me it's because the blue lobster could smell the lobster bait he had put into the trap." Nicholas remembered the awful smell that came out of Hap's lobster bait barrel. Old, salted fish—Yuck! But the lobsters loved it.

Hap announced that this blue lobster was too rare to eat and he was going to send it to the National Aquarium in Washington, D.C. They had extra big aquariums there. Hap knew they would take good care of his blue lobster. Lobsters can live to be fifty years old, you know. The aquarium would give Hap a big cash bonus for his catch. He was super happy about that, too.

Today was a special day for Hap when he found the blue lobster in his pot. He would remember this day for a long time, and he was glad his fishermen friends were there to **celebrate** with him.

Things slowly settled down on the big fishing dock. Nicholas and John walked over to visit the Captain on his fishing boat. The Captain told them that hundreds of years ago in Europe, lobsters were considered peasant food and the rich people wouldn't eat them. Instead, they fed them to prisoners. Sometimes they were used for fertilizer.

Nicholas thought, "I love the taste of lobster when Hap gives me a bite. I think those old European people and some early American settlers were missing out. Lobsters cooked for dinner are a delicious treat."

It was getting late in the afternoon. All the tourists, camera men and TV people had left the dock. Nicholas gave one more check around the big fishing dock to be sure the mice were not near the fish nets drying on the dock. The seagulls had stayed away because there were so many people around. Good thing! "Imagine if a seagull had dropped a quahog on one of the tourists. That would certainly have made the news!" Nicholas laughed.

Time to head back to the little park, check on his Mom, and then climb back onto his favorite branch for a nice snooze. Tomorrow would be another workday for Nicholas on the big fishing dock. He hoped tomorrow would be quieter! No more blue lobsters! Nevertheless, he would be ready.

After all that was his job.

A RAINY DAY

Time for work. Time for work. But it was raining! Nicholas the cat did not like the rain or getting wet—which always happened when it rained! Cats are good swimmers but they don't want to swim. Swimming means getting wet! "To be avoided at all times!" Nicholas knew.

Nicholas's job was to help all the fishermen on the big fishing dock. He kept the mice away and chased the seagulls off the boat decks. Not allowed! Not allowed! Ever! But today it was raining.

Nicholas knew that rainy days on the big fishing dock were boring. Rainy days on the fishing dock were dreary. Rainy days on the dock were lonely. The fishermen didn't take their boats out in bad weather. No one came to pet him or scratch his ears. He missed that. He missed working with the fishermen. After all, that was his job.

His first job was to chase those pesky mice. Nicholas kept them from chewing on the fish nets and biting holes in them as they sat drying on the dock. The Captain did not need a hole in his net as he was towing it to catch fish. Think of all the fish escaping through a hole!

Because of the rain, however, all the mice were hiding where it was dry, so he didn't have to chase them. Boring!

Nicholas's second job was controlling the seagulls. When seagulls managed to catch a fish or crab nearby, they would head for the fishing boats. They looked at the boat decks as their

private dining room tables. A great place to eat their lunch. What a mess! No seagulls on the boats! Nicholas had to keep them away.

However, this rainy day, Nicholas couldn't chase the seagulls. They loved the rain and were paddling happily around in the harbor.

Nicholas saw the Captain's red truck on the dock. "Great. That means the Captain is probably working on his boat. Someone for me to visit," thought Nicholas.

He and the Captain were good friends. The Captain worked hard to keep his boat and fish nets in good condition. He was always fixing something. "Safety first," Nicholas had heard the Captain say many times. The Captain's big fishing boat was designed to tow a big fish net. The net caught lots and lots of fish in it with one tow.

Nicholas could hear that the Captain's radio was playing music. Cats have amazing hearing, you know. Music was an interesting thing to Nicholas. Sometimes it was loud and sometimes soft. Sometimes people were singing and sometimes no one was singing. Nicholas didn't understand how all that music could come out of one small box. He wondered where all those singers were hiding.

The Captain saw Nicholas on the dock in the rain and invited him to come into the boat's cabin where he would be warm and dry. He knew how much cats liked cozy, warm places and not wet, drizzly places.

Nicholas and the Captain had become great friends. One day when Nicholas was taking a catnap in the cabin of the boat, he had heard a noise. The noise kept getting louder and louder and as Nicholas explored inside the cabin, he discovered a leak! Nicholas sent out an alarm and the Captain had come quickly and repaired the leak. Nicholas had *"saved the day"* and the Captain's boat. They were 'besties' after that.

"A rainy day is a good day to repair a net," the Captain told Nicholas, "and I've been doing it for many years." The Captain would be ready to fish again when the weather improved. He loved driving his big boat out to sea to fish.

Nicholas was a good friend. He curled up in the Captain's cabin and 'purred' along with the music on the radio. The Captain was happy to see Nicholas so content. The day turned out to be a happy rainy day for both of them.

AHAB AND OLD IRONSIDES

Toward the end of summer, Nicholas noticed that all the villagers were talking about one thing--there was going to be a parade of the tall ships. He knew that tall ships are large, classic sailing vessels. These ships are about forty feet long with many masts and riggings. Although they are too big to come into Nicholas's harbor or to the big fishing dock, he hoped the Captain would take him out in his boat to watch the tall ships parade.

Wow! The Captain did invite Hannah and her family to watch the tall ships parade and Nicholas was included, of course. The Captain had *saved the day!*

Nicholas heard Eva, Hannah's Mom, tell her of a special ship she had visited in Boston when she was attending culinary school. She was studying to be a pastry chef.

Eva had received an invitation to visit a special ship and wanted to take Hannah along. She told Hannah that the ship was named the *USS CONSTITUTION*. It had been named by President George Washington. This tall ship was built and berthed in Boston, Massachusetts. The ship was launched in 1797, over 200 years ago. Nicholas learned that the ship's nickname is Old Ironsides. Why? Because this frigate had successfully defeated and sunk five British warships without being harmed. That had earned her the nickname Old Ironsides!

"Could Nicholas come, too?" Hannah asked her Mom? Because Nicholas was a trained therapy cat, Eva knew he would wear his harness and walk on his leash, so her Mom said, "Yes!" Off they went.

Hannah's Mom taught her that, "Old Ironsides was made of wood and had three masts. This ship is a heavy frigate and belongs to the U.S. Navy. It is the oldest commissioned naval

vessel still afloat. When it was in service, it protected merchant ships and defeated pirates. Big cannons armed this ship.

Although it is an active Navy ship, it is old and now serves as a training ship and offers educational programs. The *USS CONSTITUTION* is open to visitors and offers free tours." Hannah could not wait to get on board.

Eva went on to explain that their visit today was more than a casual visit to this old ship. Today was retirement day for a friend of her Mom's. Any Naval officer retiring from service can request to have his or her retirement ceremony performed on Old Ironsides. This is a formal ceremony. Eva was looking forward to seeing her old friend who would be retiring.

Hannah watched as Nicholas was welcomed onto Old Ironsides with a salute. Nicholas could tell that Hannah was surprised at the size of this ship. She figured, "Nothing this big ever came to the big fishing dock where Nicholas worked." Hannah and Nicholas walked around the ship and inspected where the sixty sailors who lived on board cooked and slept. They saw the huge cannons used to fight the enemy.

Something caught Nicholas's eye. What is that? A huge animal appeared on the deck! This creature was so big that Nicholas wasn't sure what it was. It raced toward Nicholas at a full gallop and almost knocked him over. Nicholas didn't have time to think or move.

Once Nicholas caught his breath, he stared at the huge cat! It was purring and rubbing up against Nicholas.

This cat is big! Nicholas could tell he was muscular and he had long, long fur. "His coat is silky the same as mine," realized Nicholas. "His fur has many colors of browns and gold all mixed together."

Nicholas could tell that the huge cat was surprised and happy to have another cat on his ship. Nicholas was also surprised!

The big cat looked at Nicholas and said, "My name is Ahab." After a few minutes, Ahab and Nicholas became great friends.

Nicholas saw Ahab go right up to Hannah. Remember, Hannah is only five years old. He watched Ahab rub against her legs and then raise up on his hind legs. Ahab stretched out and could actually put his front paws up on Hannah's shoulders. He rubbed his face against Hannah's. Eva had to hold Hannah so Ahab didn't tip her over. Nicholas saw a delighted smile cover Hannah's face.

Ahab was the biggest cat Nicholas had ever seen. He learned that Ahab lived on Old Ironsides and was the ship's mascot. His job was to keep the mice away the same as Nicholas did on his big fishing dock. Nicholas learned that cats are always welcome on large ships. Ahab was a Maine Coon cat and his breed was brought into New England by sailors many years ago.

Maine Coon cats are gentle and love to play. They need lots of exercise. Nicholas knew a good mouser had to be fast, and Ahab was fast! He liked to race around the ship all the time. The sailors on board would hear him coming and would duck out of the way. He was like a tornado when he ran. Because of his size, he was also known for knocking things over.

Nicholas could tell that Ahab wondered why Nicholas couldn't run around the ship with him. Nicholas explained that he was a therapy cat and had to wear his harness and leash when he was out and about. That was all right with Ahab. Nicholas knew that Ahab was excited to have a cat on his ship.

Nicholas invited Ahab to stay with him and Hannah's family throughout the retirement ceremony. Nicholas sat down and Ahab joined him. Nicholas told him that it was an important time and they should stay quiet.

However, once the ceremony was over, Ahab had to get into the act. Nicholas watched him prance around and greet everyone. "What a special cat," thought Nicholas. "I wonder if he ever slows down!"

Nicholas felt a little sad when Hannah's family said it was time to go home. He knew Hannah had learned a lot about one of the oldest tall ships called Old Ironsides. Nicholas had learned a lot about Maine Coon cats, too, especially one named Ahab. What a day!

As Eva drove them home, Nicholas knew he would always remember the big Maine Coon cat named Ahab. Who could forget that! Now it was time to get home and check on things on the big fishing dock. Nicholas had had an exciting day in Boston, but his job was waiting for him. A final check of things on the dock at the end of the day was a must. The mice and seagulls had to be kept away from the boats. Nicholas wanted to be sure all his fishermen friends had returned to the dock and were safe after a day of fishing. After all, that was his job.

A SUNNY DAY – VETERAN'S DAY

Nicholas woke to a wonderful sunny morning. He had had a good night's sleep snuggled up with his Mom. He missed snuggling up with his sister, but she had recently been adopted by a wonderful family who lived nearby. He hoped she would come by for a visit soon. The Johnson twins were taking good care of his sister Misty, but he still missed her every day.

Nicholas loved the change of seasons in New England. Spring, summer, fall then winter—each season was exciting. Nicholas liked the spring season when the trees sprouted new leaves and the snow melted away. He noticed the children didn't have to bundle up with heavy winter coats as they enjoyed the spring weather. All the trees opened up to beautiful flowers. The apple blossoms smelled sweet as he strolled by.

Summer arrived later with hot breezes and a chance to play outdoors. New England summers could be quite warm, hot and humid. Following that, fall arrived with its crisp, cool air. The sun was still warm and there was still a hint of summer in the air.

It was now fall in New England, and mornings were cooler. Leaves were turning beautiful gold and red colors. There was a hint of winter coming. Winter, of course, was cold! Icy rain! Snow! Great, if you liked to ski.

But today was a wonderful fall day; a great day to play and explore. *Nicholas was good at that!*

Things on the big fishing dock were quiet this Sunday morning. Sundays were almost like a vacation day for Nicholas with his job of keeping the mice away from the fish nets that were stacked on the big fishing dock. Nicholas was fast as he chased the mice away. That was his job! How was his best friend, the Captain of a big fishing boat, going to catch fish if his nets had holes in them?

Nicholas also had to keep his eye on the seagulls. Seagulls were special birds but could make a mess on the fishing boats and that was not allowed! Nicholas would make a quick leap, and scare the gulls away. Although these birds were bigger than Nicholas, he knew how to do his job. He let them know he was the boss of the big fishing dock.

Nicholas took a stroll around the fishing dock one more time to check on the mice and seagull situation. All was quiet so he knew he could relax and play for a little while.

He went up the street to visit his friend Hannah, but she and her Mom and Dad were in church. Mr. Brown and his whole family were in church, too. Mr. Brown's lovely cat, Sophia, was in the house and couldn't come out to play. Their dog Lassie was in his dog house and wasn't interested in playing with Nicholas either.

Nicholas had already learned not to bother their goat. The goat liked to butt Nicholas with his head and toss him into the air. It never hurt, but it wasn't fun either!

Nicholas wandered back to the park near the fishing dock, but no one was there. "Gosh. I don't have anyone to play with. Where is everyone?" wondered Nicholas.

Nicholas decided to meander up the street to the shopping village to see if anything was going on. He noticed the village was extra busy. American flags were flying up and down the street in their special holders. People were beginning to gather on the sidewalks with their families. They were happy as they met with their friends enjoying the sun. There was music playing from a truck nearby. A man with a special curly mustache was playing patriotic songs. The old timers called his mustache a 'handlebar' mustache. You could hear the music all over the village.

Today was Veteran's Day! He had almost forgotten that his Mom had told him there was going to be a parade today. "How could I have forgotten!" thought Nicholas. "That's why people are gathering on the sidewalks. They are waiting for the parade!"

Nicholas's Mom had taught him, "Always thank the soldiers for their service to the country. Veteran's Day is a special day created for that purpose--to remember all of the present day soldiers and those from the past who had served our country.

"At the end of World War I, a peace treaty was signed on the 11th hour of the 11th day of the 11th month. Veteran's Day is always **celebrated** on November 11 for that reason. This year it happened to be on a Sunday."

Nicholas managed to find a spot at the top of some stairs where he could see what was going on. There were lots of children around and they all wanted to play with him. He loved to have them scratch his ears and it was all right with him if they wanted to pick him up and give him a hug.

Pretty soon Nicholas saw a police car coming down the street with all its lights flashing. It *wasn't* an emergency! The **celebration** was starting! The police car was leading the start of the whole parade. Next came some soldiers marching in their smart looking uniforms. There was a military band, too. The soldiers kept in perfect step to the beat of the band music. He saw that Hannah's Dad had his uniform on and was marching with his soldier friends. He looked proud and it made Hannah and her Mom smile, clap their hands, and cheer.

Next came a group of men and women Nicholas had seen on the television once. They were important people. There was the Governor of his state, a Congressman and a Senator. The local Town Manager was marching. "I think they are called 'politicians'," Nicholas kind of laughed.

There were old antique cars in the parade. Nicholas knew that some 'old timers' would be driving these special cars. They were shiny and had funny horns that said "Ah-oo-gah! Ah-oo-gah!" Nicholas had never heard anything like it before. The sound of the horns tickled his ears.

The high school band came next. Nicholas couldn't count how many students were in that band. They wore bright blue and gold uniforms. Their tall hats had big feathers on the top.

There were clarinets, tubas, trumpets, trombones, flutes and lots and lots of drums. Nicholas's ears told him they played much louder than the military band! There was a drum major leading the band members. He wore the biggest hat of all.

There were majorettes with their shiny batons that they twirled and spun high into the air. It was exciting to watch. People cheered the band as they passed by.

Nicholas looked up as he heard a gigantic roar overhead. A big jet fighter plane suddenly flew over the parade. Jets make a lot of noise. Imagine seeing one of the country's fastest military jets flying over our heads. The children ducked because it was so loud. Nicholas jumped so high, all four paws left the ground! The jet plane was louder than fireworks or the bands.

Would you believe there were horses in the parade? Kathy, from the Santana Center, had brought four of her special horses to the parade. She and her friends were riding them. Kathy had tied ribbons to their tails and draped fresh flowers around their necks. Hannah was so excited to see Kaito, the horse she had ridden on
her first riding lesson. Hannah's Mom said, "Hannah, maybe next year you can ride Kaito in the parade." Hannah started

giggling and giggling because she was so excited to think about that.

Nicholas spotted the Captain driving his red truck. The truck was pulling a hay wagon and there were members of the adult and children's chorus riding in the wagon. They were throwing Tootsie Rolls to the crowd. Best of all, they were singing their special songs. Some of the singers were marching and waving to the crowd. People on the sidewalks started singing with them. Singing was great fun! You can't have a parade without music.

Nicholas had no idea there were so many Cub Scouts, Boy Scouts, Brownies and Girl Scouts in his little village? They carried their banners and wore all the merit badges they had earned. To remember the sailors lost at sea, they placed a wreath of flowers in the water.

Next came the firetrucks. Their lights were flashing and their sirens were blasting. The sad part is that the firetrucks marked the end of the parade.

Nicholas had had a great morning watching the parade. When he had remembered that today was Veteran's Day, he knew it was going to be a special day, and it was!

Mr. Brown had invited people who had participated in the parade to come to his yard for a free hot dog roast. The soldiers came, the scouts came, the firemen came, the policemen came, and the high school band came. Nicholas figured they would need a lot of hot dogs. He hoped he might get one bite. Best ending ever to such a special Veteran's Day.

Nicholas and Sophia, Mr. Brown's cat, did manage to share a hot dog. Nicholas liked catsup on his hot dog but Sophia thought it was too fattening! "Girls!" Nicholas smiled.

The whole village had created a special Veteran's Day. Past and present Veterans were remembered and thanked for their service. The whole village had **celebrated** and *saved the day!*

THE FARM

Nicholas always smelled something special in the air when the fall season came around. The air was crisp and cool, but there was still lots of sparkling sunshine. The maple tree leaves were beginning to turn red and gold. Soon they would cover the ground like a colorful blanket. They were beautiful to look at as long as you weren't the one who had to rake them up.

New England is busy in the fall. Nicholas was invited to visit a farm with the Captain's family where they met the owner. He was cooking on a hot grill and they watched as he prepared Johnny Cakes. He told the Captain that in the 'old days,' maybe hundreds of years ago, travelers would cook griddle cakes made of corn that had been ground into meal. When cooked, they looked something like a pancake.

They were not called Johnny Cakes many years ago, however. They were called 'Journey Cakes.' The farmer explained that the 'Journey Cakes' were easy for travelers to save and eat as they moved across the country. This was when families were traveling west to settle new territories.

Nicholas checked out the helper who was cooking the cakes. They did smell wonderful as they cooked on a big cast iron grill. The chef covered them with butter. Nicholas stayed close by in case he might get a sample.

"Now-a-days," the farmer said, "it is easy for us to buy the ground corn meal in the grocery store. I cook mine the same as the old timers did on a cast iron griddle. I cook them in bacon fat." Nicholas was thinking that they probably didn't have olive oil back in those days. The farmer must be a real 'old timer' realized Nicholas. He knew all the old tricks.

A few days later, Hannah's family, with Nicholas tagging along, visited another nearby farm where the farmer was harvesting his vegetable gardens. Shoppers could pull up the vegetables they wanted to buy right from the ground.

Hannah headed for the carrots. Nicholas watched her struggle to pull up a carrot. Harvesting the carrots was hard because they were rooted deep in the ground. She was pulling so hard that when the carrot popped out, it caused her to fall over backwards with a thump. She wasn't hurt, but surprised. Nicholas heard her giggle--that famous Hannah giggle. She got up and bent over to go after another carrot. Her Mom and Dad stood there enjoying the show!

The farmer also grew beets, cabbages, cauliflower and brussel sprouts. "Not for me," thought Nicholas. "I much prefer eating fish and meat."

There were big baskets of tomatoes and squash. Hannah's Mom, Eva, had her eye on the tomatoes because she used them to make her delicious spaghetti sauce. Jim, Hannah's Dad, helped carry the heavy basket of tomatoes to the stand.

Corn, Corn, Corn—it was everywhere. The corn grew tall, tall, and taller. The corn was almost as tall as Hannah's Dad. Nicholas took off racing through the corn fields with Hannah.

They took a right, they took a left. They took another left. Nicholas questioned, "Hmmm. Where are we now?" They took a right turn. This was getting confusing.

Hannah followed Nicholas as if he knew where he was going. Actually, Nicholas had no idea where he was in the corn field. He wasn't sure how to get back to the farm stand. About that time, Nicholas heard Hannah's Mom give a call and he and Hannah headed for her voice. Nicholas had excellent hearing and now he knew which way to go.

Hannah's Mom, who always wore her big red floppy hat, filled another basket with as many fresh vegetables as she could. "Vegetables are important. You can't eat apple pie and ice cream every night!" she said. Nicholas didn't know if he agreed with that because he always gobbled up the ice cream she always put on top.

The most fun on the farm that day was picking pumpkins. Nicholas had no idea what you would do with those big round orange things. Jim couldn't wait to get the pumpkin he chose back home so he could carve it for Halloween.

"Halloween is an old tradition and it is **celebrated** in many different ways in many different countries," Jim told Hannah. "It's a time to remember past family members and friends. In

New England, children like to dress up in costumes, visit their neighbors and hopefully, collect some candy from them."

Hannah's Mom had other plans for her pumpkin. She was going to cook it. She would remove all the seeds from the inside, cook it and mash it. She would add lots of tasty spices like cinnamon, nutmeg and cloves. Sugar, milk and eggs were added next. "Ah ha!" thought Nicholas. "I bet she's going to make another of her famous pies—pumpkin!" All their neighbors knew she made the best pies in his whole village.

When they got home from the farm, Hannah became more interested in what her Dad was doing. He cut the top off his pumpkin, and started removing all the seeds. Taking them out was a sticky, sticky job, but fun. Hannah liked getting her hands inside the pumpkin and pulling out the seeds. Her hands were sticky right up to her elbows. She kept threatening to pick up Nicholas with her sticky fingers. "Yuck! What a mess," exclaimed Nicholas as he kept his distance.

Hannah had drawn a picture of what she wanted her Halloween pumpkin's face to look like. Scary! Her Dad took a sharp knife and cut out the eyes, nose and mouth. The eyes were pointy and sharp. The nose was a triangle. The mouth was the scariest. It was crooked with raggedy teeth! They put a candle in the bottom of the carved pumpkin.

Hannah told Nicholas, "When it gets dark outside, we'll light the candle and the light will shine through the scary face. We'll put it in the front window so everyone can see it."

They were all set for Halloween. Nicholas wasn't too happy about Halloween. Children came into his little park. They were dressed in scary costumes. Some of them chased Nicholas and

pretended they were ghosts. Nicholas fled up into his favorite tree so he could hide and stay out of the way.

This year, Hannah's wanted her costume to be a princess. Her Mom made her a beautiful blue and white gown with ruffles and lace. Blue was Hannah's favorite color. Her Mom also made a crown by cutting out some cardboard and covering it with shiny silver paper.

Hannah's Mom said, "Here, Hannah. Try this on." She gave her one of her pretty necklaces. Hannah pretended it was made of diamonds and rubies and emeralds. "That's what a princess would wear," declared Hannah. She did indeed look like a princess. Hannah giggled and couldn't wait to visit her neighbors to get some treats. You know, 'trick or treat!'

Hannah's Dad took her hand and walked her down their street. When Nicholas saw Hannah and her Dad walking near the little park where he had been hiding, he jumped down from his favorite branch and decided to tag along. There were lots of other children dressed up, too. There were soldiers, nurses, ghosts, doctors—some pretty and some scary. One boy was dressed up as a clown with a big red nose and a funny wig of yellow, straggly hair.

After a walk with Hannah through their neighborhood dashing from one house to another, Nicholas was feeling a little tired. After all, he had started the day at his job on the big fishing dock followed by two busy trips to the farms.

He had *celebrated* Halloween with Hannah. He said good night to Hannah by rubbing against her legs and purring. He hoped she wouldn't eat too much candy and get a tummy ache.

Tomorrow it was back to work for Nicholas at the big fishing dock. After all, that was his job.

KINDERGARTEN

Nicholas was in serious need for some rough and tumble playing, but no one was in the park today. All his friends were beginning to think about going back to school as summer was ending.

The smell of apple pie was floating through the air and it made Nicholas think of Hannah. Her Mom was a professional baker. Apple pie with ice cream (but only ice cream for Nicholas) was so delicious. So he trotted up the street to Hannah's house.

Hannah was excited to see Nicholas and she wanted to show him the new desk her Mom had bought for her. She told Nicholas that she was getting ready to go to kindergarten in

September. "Kindergarten? School?" wondered Nicholas. He knew Hannah was five years old. Was she ready to go to school? Kindergarten classes help children get ready for first grade. Kindergarten is for four to six year old children. The word is based on a German word: *Kinder* means children, and *Garten* means garden. Put those two words together and you get *kindergarten*.

Hannah loved to play school. Sometimes she was the student, sometimes she was the teacher, and sometimes she pretended that she was the parent.

Today she told Nicholas that he was going to be the student, and she was going to be the teacher. He climbed up onto the chair of her new desk. Hannah told him to "sit still and pay attention!" He sat still as Hannah told him, "Today class, we are going play a game. This game is called the 'sharing' game. I'm going to give you a ball and you have to share it with someone else in the class." Nicholas knew that he was the only 'student' in the room, so he wasn't sure how this game was going to work.

Hannah put a small red ball on top of Nicholas's desk. Nicholas took a swing at it with his paw and it bounced off the desk onto the floor and ended up in the lap of Hannah's favorite toy bear, Humphrey. "Good job!" exclaimed Hannah. "You shared the ball with Humphrey, my toy bear. Now you have to ask the bear if he will give it back to you. Do you think the bear with share the ball with you?"

Nicholas listened carefully, but he had no idea. He sat by Humphrey the bear and took his paw and tapped on the ball and made it roll back to the desk. He wasn't able to pick it up, of course, but Hannah did it for him. Nicholas got a gold star for sharing.

Now it was snack time. Snack time at school was always delicious, especially if your Mom baked special desserts. Today the snack was an oatmeal raisin cookie for Hannah and a 'pretend' cookie for Nicholas. "Pretend cookie? What kind of a snack is that!" thought Nicholas. He liked real snacks like a taste of chowder or a piece of fish or chicken. That was a snack!

Hannah was still playing the teacher. "Now class, its rest time." Hannah climbed up on her bed and Nicholas jumped up too and sat on her pillow. Before long, Hannah was taking a nap. "School wasn't as hard as I thought it would be," Nicholas realized.

Enough school for one day! Besides, he needed to check on how things were going on the big fishing dock.

He quietly climbed down from Hannah's bed and headed back to the big fishing dock. Between looking out for mice and seagulls, it was a never ending chore. But after all, that was his job.

HURRICANE

When Nicholas woke up this morning, he could feel that there was a change in the air. Something was different. Something was happening. It wasn't foggy with dew dripping off the tree branches, and it wasn't raining. The air was humid. When there is a high level of humidity in the air, the air feels thick and the air is warm at the same time. And it was; the air was quiet and heavy.

　The sky was thick with clouds that hung low in the sky. They were not the white fluffy clouds that you see on a sunny day. Not even close. These clouds were flat, slow moving, and threatening.

Nicholas walked over to the big fishing dock. There was a lot of activity going on. Everyone was rushing around. Why?

NOAA (National Oceanic & Atmospheric Administration) had put up the hurricane flags!

A hurricane! A hurricane was approaching. Nicholas saw the special flags flying over the dock. There is no other flag like a hurricane flag, and when it is flown, seamen know what they have to do.

Nicholas had heard the fishermen talking about bad weather approaching. The fishermen had been talking about it for days. The storm had formed into an actual hurricane yesterday with winds over seventy-four miles per hour. Now it had taken a turn toward New England. The big fishing dock where Nicholas worked was in the storm's path.

A hurricane meant many things—most of them not good!

Hap, Nicholas's lobsterman friend, was warming up his engine to go to sea and haul out all of his lobster pots. He knew that

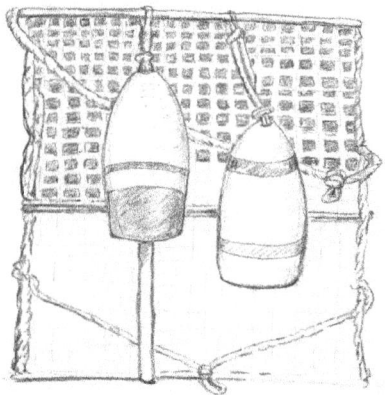

thanks to the hurricane warning, he had enough time to get to sea and pull his lobster pots and buoys out of the water.

With high winds and extra high seas, Hap's lobster pots could be ripped up and washed ashore and smashed--including the new metal pots. Catching lobsters was Hap's business and he knew he had to collect and protect his lobster gear.

Hap also knew he had to remove those awful smelly barrels of lobster bait stored on the dock. Although the lobsters were attracted to the awful bait that Hap put in his pots, Nicholas knew to stay away from the barrels. Ugh! Yuck! Phew! But, the lobsters loved it. Again, the high, rough seas would tip the barrels over onto the dock, wash them overboard, and sink them.

The Captain was also busy removing all his nets that were sitting on the dock. He was putting them into the back of his red truck. The Captain used many different sized nets depending on what type of fish he was towing for. The dock would be under water and his nets would be destroyed by the large waves that rolled in with a hurricane.

Anything that was left on the dock would be washed away. All the fishermen had to save their fishing gear.

A tidal surge happens when a hurricane comes near. Strong winds push the water ahead of the storm and up onto the land. This sudden flood can wipe out homes and businesses if they are located near the water's edge.

The USS Coast Guard had already warned all vessels to seek safe harbor before the hurricane got too close. They let all ships and residents know how hard the wind would blow and how much flooding there would be. Large ships at sea also had to change course and get away from the travelling hurricane.

In Nicholas's village, the local police go to each home in any area that might be flooded. They advise the residents to leave and take their pets with them. There are shelters provided for these residents in different areas of the village. Residents remove anything in their yards that might blow around and cause damage. Stores and home owners sometimes boarded up their windows for extra protection.

A tree might fall on a house; windows might be broken. That doesn't matter. What matters is that everyone gets to safety.

The Captain knew that the only way to save his big boat was to ride out the storm. Riding out a storm could be dangerous. The Captain knew that once the hurricane arrived with its high tides and strong winds, he would be ready to move his boat to a safer place. Tied up to the dock was not safe for him or his boat.

The Captain knew of a small cove nearby that would offer a lot of protection from the wind and rough water. Usually there wouldn't be enough water in the cove to bring in a big boat like the Captain's, but with the tidal surge, the Captain knew that it would be deep enough for him to drive his boat there for a while.

He also knew it would only be safe until the eye of the hurricane passed. When that happened, the wind and tide changed direction, and it changed fast. The water would rush out of the cove. He would have to get his boat out of the small cove in a hurry or his boat would go ashore. Would he anchor his boat in the cove? No. The Captain had to keep his boat running and hold it into the wind so it wouldn't be blown ashore or onto some rocks. He would run his engine enough to keep the boat

held steady into the wind. He had to stay alert the whole time keeping his eye on the wind and tide.

The Captain was following the weather reports constantly on his radio to keep track of the hurricane.

Boats that were moored in the harbor had prepared by tying on a second line to add strength to their mooring. Still many of them might be cut free by the fierce wind. They would end up on the shore. The boat owners did not have time to get all their vessels hauled out of the water.

Nicholas was thinking of John, his favorite shell fisherman. He knew that John's boat, although it was powerful and fast, was the right size to be hauled out of the water onto a boat trailer. He would drive it to safer ground. John's house was right on the beach near the fish market. He could walk from his home to his boat when he was heading to work catching quahogs.

John knew to bring his boat trailer to what is called a launching ramp. In the summer, boaters that have their small boats on trailers can roll them into the water where they float off. Now it was the opposite.

John backed his boat trailer into the water and drove his skiff onto it. His truck pulled the trailer out of the water and John parked his skiff in a safe place away from the wind and rising water.

Nicholas was watching all the fishermen prepare for what could be a very, very terrible and destructive storm. He noticed that there were no seagulls in the sky. They weren't swimming in the harbor either. The seagulls knew it would be safer for them to fly to a sheltered place. They might head into a wooded area where it would not be so windy.

Nicholas also looked around the big fishing dock for the mice that sometimes got into trouble chewing on the Captain's fish nets. Nicholas was concerned about one little mouse named Tim who had become his friend. He wanted to know he would be safe. Animals can often detect that bad weather is coming, and know how to protect themselves. That includes the little mice. There wasn't a mouse in sight.

The nearby fish market also had lots to do to get ready for the hurricane. They had a large generator sitting up high on a bench in case water came into the building. After all, the fish market was sitting at the end of a dock surrounded by water.

The generator would make electricity if the power went out. The lobsters that were kept alive in the market's sea water tanks needed constant fresh sea water pumped into them. The fish market also had fish stored in big refrigerators that had to be kept cold. Generators would provide the electricity. The most important thing was that all the helpers at the market were sent home to be safe with their families.

As the storm grew closer, The Captain, Nicholas's best friend, was happy to know that Nicholas and his Mom were going to stay at Mr. Smith's house with his nine children and nine pets. Their son's dog named Lassie liked Nicholas and his Mom, so there would be no cat-dog problems! Sophie their cat was delighted to have Nicholas in her home so they could play.

Mr. Smith moved Lassie's dog house into his garage. The parakeet cage that had been hanging on the porch was brought inside, too. Things that weren't tied down had to be moved to safety. There was a lot of work to be done, but preparations were extremely important.

Mrs. Smith did some cooking ahead of time in case they lost electric power. Of course, they could always have tuna fish sandwiches. Nicholas knew that that would an excellent idea. Yum!

Nicholas also began to think about his special friend Hannah. For safety's sake, Jim and Eva, her parents, had secured their little cottage and moved to a shelter. They hoped Eva's baking equipment would not be damaged. Jim had moved Hannah's doll house from their back yard into her room. You never knew if the wind would break a window and rain would pour in and do damage. Storms brought many, many troubles. Especially hurricanes!

Nicholas knew that his little sister, Misty, would be safe in the big yellow house with the Johnson family who had adopted her.

Nicholas also knew that there was one special thing about hurricanes, and it was a *good* thing. The Captain had explained to Nicholas that thanks to NOAA, the USS Coast Guard, the local and national weather bureaus, and the local television and radio stations, that people were *warned* that a hurricane was coming. In other words, it gave the villagers time to prepare. No one living by the sea ignored warnings about a possible hurricane arriving. No one!

Nicholas realized how dangerous it would be to live where tornadoes dropped down out of the sky without giving much warning or time to prepare.

He felt comfortable that good preparations had been made around him on the big fishing dock and for all his friends. The Captain's family was safe in their large home that sat away from the harbor.

The hurricane was coming. Nicholas with his extraordinary hearing could hear the wind begin to pick up and blow harder. His Mom sat on a windowsill watching the leaves blow around Mr. Smith's yard. The trees were beginning to bend with the wind.

Nicholas had seen the Captain leave the dock and steer his boat to the nearby safe cove. Nicholas had to trust that all would be well.

He knew that Hap had picked up all his lobster pots and buoys. John, the shell fisherman, had taken all his cats with him and moved to a shelter with Hannah's family.

Signs of the hurricane storm were starting and families tried to keep busy. The children played indoor games and the adults listened to the latest weather reports. Candles were ready to be lit in case the electricity stopped. Some people had old fashioned kerosene lanterns that would give off light if they lost power.

Those were the real 'old timers.'

Now it was time to wait.

BEAUTIFUL SUNRISE

Nicholas had often heard about "the calm before the storm," but in this case, following the hurricane, it was the calm *after* the storm. He couldn't wait to get outside and down to the big fishing dock to check on all the fishermen.

Nicholas noticed that it was quiet outside. The sun was shining and the air moved gently around him. You'd think it was a perfect summer morning, except it was the morning after a hurricane and nothing about that was normal.

The hurricane had passed and it had been a strong storm--a category four. Nicholas and his Mom had stayed with the Smith family up the street from the big fishing dock. Their house was well built and sturdy. Only minor damage had been done from branches hitting the side of the house. No windows were broken. All the shingles were still attached to the roof.

The goat was safe in the garage as well as the chickens. Mr. Smith had made sure there was nothing close by that the goat might decide to chew on. He left him some carrots to keep him busy. Mr. Smith had created a small wire mesh cage for the chickens in the garage. They didn't seem to mind the wind at all and kept pecking at their grain.

Electric power had gone off some time in the evening as the hurricane hit. The wind and falling trees had cut down power lines. The repairmen had worked all night during the storm, and power was restored by morning. The power repair trucks had driven to Nicholas's area before the storm hit so they would be ready to get repairs done quickly. Amazing!

Without electricity, the Smith family had built a pretend campfire in their fireplace. They ate cereal with fruit and told each other stories--some funny, some scary. Nicholas began thinking, "We don't need scary stories what with the wind howling so hard outside!" He kept thinking and worrying about the Captain riding out the storm in his boat.

This morning it was finally safe to go outside. The hurricane had moved north and away from Nicholas's village. People were out and about checking on their properties. Some trees were down and small branches and leaves were everywhere. The leaves stuck to the sides of the houses and they almost looked like wallpaper. They had to be rinsed off. You had to watch where you walked or you might trip on branches, sticks, and small objects like garden pots that had not been stored away.

Everything that was not 'tied down,' as the old timers would say, had blown all over the yards. Salt spray from the harbor had also sprayed many of the homes near the water and that also had to be hosed off.

Nicholas's Mom walked with Nicholas back to the park to see how all the children's slides, swings and their little merry-go-round had survived. They both saw that the tide had come up so high that it had covered the big fishing dock with a few feet of water which, of course, went right into the nearby park. Things in the park were in place, but needed to be cleaned. Some fishing gear and old lobster pots had washed up into the park.

Nicholas's favorite tree had survived although there weren't many leaves left on the branches. He knew they would grow back.

When the hurricane came in, it blew tons of water in ahead of it which had covered the dock. As Nicholas headed to the big fishing dock, he could see where the tide had come up into the road leaving piles of seaweed and debris in its wake.

Some of the smaller skiffs that had been tied to the dock were now sitting on top of it. Others were sunk. Sometimes it is better for a small boat to sink rather than be crashed onto the dock. All could be repaired.

Nicholas's biggest relief came when he saw the Captain's boat tied back up to the big fishing dock in his special spot. He and his boat had survived the hurricane. Nicholas made a bee-line to greet him.

The Captain was extremely tired from riding out the storm all night, but he greeted Nicholas with a big hug, and lots of ear scratching. There was lots of purring from Nicholas, too! The Captain and Nicholas walked around the big fishing dock talking with the other fishermen to see if there was damage, and what they could do to help.

Everyone was safe! Some boats were lost and some fishing gear was missing, but that didn't matter. All the fishermen were safe!

The biggest tragedy, however, happened to Hap's lobster boat. There was such a huge surge of water that lifted his boat way above the dock. When the eye of the hurricane passed, the water quickly receded. Hap's boat had landed on top of one of the pilings on the dock. The piling went right through the bottom of the boat!

Fishermen are resourceful and Hap was a good carpenter as well as a lobsterman. He knew he could get a crane to lift the boat off the piling and he could repair the hole. What a job! Hap knew all his fishermen friends would help.

Once Nicholas was sure that his fishermen friends were all right, he walked around his neighborhood to see how all his cat and dog friends had made out. All their owners had kept their pets safe inside, of course, but now they were out and about and playing as if the hurricane had never happened. Especially the dogs. They had a great time picking up all the small branches and racing around with them. Nicholas kept his distance.

Nicholas walked along the beach to see how John's house had faired. It almost sat right on the beach. John was there looking over the damage. He had returned this morning with his cats. He was lucky that no sea water got into the house, only a little rain from a broken window. The worst thing he had to worry about was that some of the smaller boats tied up in the harbor had broken loose from their moorings. One sailboat had broken loose and was within a foot of breaking into John's front door!

There were dozens of small skiffs that were blown off their moorings. If they had landed on a sandy beach there wasn't much damage. If they landed on the rocky areas, there was a lot of damage.

Next door to John's house, Nicholas saw that an old colonial house had a big tree that had crashed into the roof. Neighbors helped cover the open areas of the roof so no rain could get in and do more damage.

Young men were wandering the streets with chain saws. Nicholas could hear all the 'buzzing' noise. When they saw a large branch down, the men offered to cut it up so it could be removed. They were being helpful, of course, but Nicholas decided they might be making a little money, too!

Next he headed to Hannah's house. Her Mom had a bakery shop in their house. The wind had blown so hard that some of her pots and pans that had been hooked to the kitchen wall were shaken down and were all over the floor. Quite a mess. The chimney had also been knocked over and there were bricks laying on the roof and on the ground. The chimney would have to be rebuilt. But, the family was safe!

Hannah met John at the shelter and got to play with his three cats! Yes, they allowed people to bring their pets to the shelter. Good thing! Eva and Jim were happy that the cats kept Hannah busy so she would not worry about the strength of the storm outside. Jim had grown up in Wyoming and they didn't have hurricanes there. He had no idea what to expect and, therefore, was quite nervous for his family and their home.

All's well that ends well!

There were still some areas of the village without power, but volunteers were already driving around with water and food for the villagers until the power was turned back on.

Nicholas noticed that the seagulls were returning to the harbor. Birds know when a storm has passed. Of course, that meant that Nicholas had to get back to his job of protecting the fleet from the messy gulls and keeping the mice from chewing on the fish nets. The Captain had brought all his fish nets back onto the dock getting ready for more fishing. "Hmmm. I wonder if the mice know about that," thought Nicholas.

The villagers were **celebrating** that the storm had passed and everyone was fine. It was time for Nicholas to get back to work on the big fishing dock. After all, that was his job.

ALEX IN POLYNESIA

Nicholas heard that his old friend Alex the cat was returning to the fishing village. Alex's family were professors at the local university and they studied different cultures all over the world. They return to Nicholas's village each summer and Nicholas was looking forward to seeing his friend. He realized Alex was a lucky cat to get to visit new places all around the world.

Alex went to South America last year and had amazed Nicholas with stories of the people he met in the different villages. One village had a rescued baby elephant that liked to pick Alex up with his trunk!

This year, Alex had hoped his family would be traveling to Hawaii. Nicholas couldn't wait to her what stories Alex would tell him this summer.

Nicholas was having a good night's sleep on his favorite branch in his favorite tree. To surprise Nicholas, Alex silently climbed up and pounced on the sleeping Nicholas who woke up with a jolt! What? What a surprise! Alex was back!

The two friends chased each other down the tree and raced around the swing set and the little merry-go-round in the park. That started a morning of games between the two old friends—chasing, tumbling and pouncing on one another as only good friends can do.

Alex let Nicholas know that the family didn't get to Hawaii after all, but it was close. Halfway between Hawaii and Australia is a tiny, tiny country called Tuvalu. It is one of the smallest countries in the whole world. That was the reason that Alex's family wanted to study how it had developed. Tuvalu is located in Polynesia, the same as Hawaii, so Alex was glad to learn that it would be warm and tropical.

Alex told Nicholas, "The country of Tuvalu is made up of three reef islands and six atolls which are coral reefs that are surrounded by water. The whole country is about ten miles long which is much smaller than Nicholas's village. More people live in Nicholas's village than live in the whole country of Tuvalu.

The early Polynesian people were great sea travelers and they discovered the Tuvalu islands over three thousand years ago.

The professors found that these islands had been explored over the years by many countries including Spain, Britain, Russia and the Dutch. Whalers from Nantucket, Massachusetts also made stops to this small island country.

Tuvalu joined the United Nations in 1978, a long time before either Nicholas or Alex were born. In World War II, the islanders helped build an airfield for the American pilots. Because the islanders were such good seamen, they had helped train the Marine cadets in ways of the sea. Alex said that although the country was small, he learned how much they had given to the world.

Alex told Nicholas that the largest city was called Funafuti. He said, "Try saying that name three times fast! I got to go fishing in one of their single outrigger canoes. I never tasted a fish I didn't like." Nicholas laughed. "I couldn't believe it when the fishermen used butterfly nets to catch the flying fish! They also knew the trick of shining a spotlight into the water to attract fish. They were clever fishermen," Alex said.

"I watched them play volleyball but would you believe the balls were made out of leaves? In their volleyball game, the balls are never allowed to hit the ground. Football was also a favorite sport. Who knew!"

"When it comes to fun, mention the word *fetele*, which is their dance for special occasions. Watch the party begin! I tried to dance with the children but they were too fast for me," Alex said.

The professors learned that the islands depend a great deal on fish for their diet and their coconut woodlands for building homes. Their islands are also facing rising sea level problems today just as other countries are around the world. Their islands may be covered with water in about 100 years. What a loss that will be.

They have fresh water ponds but in some places, since the islands are made up of porous volcanic rock, sea water is seeping up into their fresh water.

Nicholas said, "I'm so surprised that your family found this tiny, tiny country, but it is a real country and has a wonderful history and people."

Alex explained that for fun the professors had asked their computer to show them tiny countries. That is how they found Tuvalu! That discovery made them curious as to how the tiny country grew and survived.

Again, Alex talked about where his family might travel and study next year. The new country was always a surprise. Alex always looked forward to returning to Nicholas's fishing village in

the summer where he could play with his old friend. He liked to help Nicholas chase the mice and seagulls on the big fishing Watch out Nicholas! Here he comes! Alex pounced on Nicholas once more. The chase is on. After all, what are friends for!

FAREWELLS

As Nicholas was beginning to doze off for a catnap, he could tell that summer was coming to a close. That meant for one thing, his friend Alex would be leaving soon for foreign adventures with his family, the Spencers. They were both professors at the local university and their specialty was studying different cultures in many countries all over the world.

Nicholas had a feeling of heaviness thinking about Alex leaving for another whole year. There were always changes going on in Nicholas's world. His sister had been adopted and moved out of the park. The good news was that she now lived nearby in the big yellow house. When she came to visit, they attacked each other as only sisters and brothers and closest of friends can. But it wasn't the same. Now Alex would be leaving soon, too.

John the shell fisherman was still his best buddy, especially when he cooked all those delicious fish recipes. Hap, the lobsterman, was always around, too, so Nicholas couldn't complain too much about being alone and maybe feeling a little lonely. Nicholas only had to show up at the big fishing dock for all kinds of friends and visitors to greet him. But Alex was a little different. They had grown up together.

Nicholas asked Alex where the professors would be travelling this year. The professors hadn't decided yet, so it would be a surprise for Alex and Nicholas. They always took special care of Alex when they were flying and traveling around the world. What an adventure.

Alex was thinking about all the vaccinations he would need to get in order to travel to a distant country. He hoped it would be warm like Tuvalu.

Next summer when Alex returned, Nicholas was sure Alex would have lots of adventures to share.

Nicholas also learned that the new tour boat was sailing its last two tours next week. That meant that Nicholas's new friend, Ned, would be heading off to college. Ned's singing made the tour guests smile. Nicholas was impressed with how much Ned knew about sea shanties. Ned had been accepted into the music program at the local university. He would be busy with his college studies, but he was also a performer and when he was singing locally, he promised to let the Captain and Nicholas know so they could come to his shows.

Nicholas rubbed against the Captain's legs and the Captain bent down to scratch his ears as he headed for his nice, warm cabin. The feeling of heaviness faded away as this was a happy time for Nicholas. That motor noise started up in Nicholas's throat. He didn't understand why that happened when he was feeling happy.

Nicholas's friend, Tom the tomcat, tried to explain that it was called 'purring.' Nicholas wondered if all cats made that fuzzy, purring sound. Tom the Tomcat who was an old friend of Nicholas's explained that yes, when cats are feeling happy and

safe, they liked to purr. Nicholas always felt happy and safe when he was around the Captain

Tom the tomcat had taught Nicholas how to help the fishermen by training him to chase the mice away and keep the seagulls off the boats. Tom was retired now, but Nicholas was always happy when he came by to visit him on the big fishing dock. After all, Tom had trained Nicholas to take over as 'boss' of the fishing dock.

"I wonder if he's checking up on me?" wondered Nicholas. "Nah, he's my best friend. He trusts me to get the job done."

Nicholas saw Tom the tomcat curled up in the tightest ball in his favorite sunny spot in the back corner of the park. He looked so content, it made Nicholas smile.

There would be changes coming up, of course, what with Alex off to his worldwide travels, and Ned off to college. Both would be missed but Nicholas knew he would be seeing them again next summer.

John, the chef and shell fisherman, was always at his boat first thing in the morning getting ready to head out to his fishing grounds. Nicholas could always count on that and on the special treats John brought him from his kitchen.

There's Hap--red t-shirt and hat on backwards as usual. He also was loading pots onto his boat getting ready to set them out at the lobster grounds. Remember that blue lobster he caught last season? Wow! Was that ever exciting. TV and Newspaper people were all over the dock. Although lobster season slowed down over the cold winter, Hap was always checking on his boat and preparing for the next lobster season. He had a special way of scratching Nicholas's ears and tickling his paws! Nicholas loved that.

His most favorite person on the big fishing dock was the Captain. He was not only his best friend, the Captain kept an eye out for his whole family. Nicholas's Mom was getting older now and she was spending more time with the Smith family up the street. They were taking special care of her and she was a great companion to Sophie, their young cat. The two of them shared sneaking naps together in the sunshine.

Nicholas knew he would always have the Captain nearby when he needed something. The Captain knew that Nicholas would always be nearby when the mice and seagulls got pesky!

REVIEW REQUEST

Thank you so much for choosing this third book in the **Nicholas the Cat** series. If you enjoyed these stories, please consider leaving a brief review online at the retailer's site where you purchased the books, on social media, or on our website (Nicholasthecat.com) to help make these books more discoverable for other readers.

ABOUT THE AUTHOR

Nicholas the Cat Celebrates is Roberta Belanger's third book in this series. She grew up and lives in Wickford, Rhode Island, a historic fishing village. It takes her five minutes to walk from her home to the big fishing dock where her father had been a commercial fisherman. The famous fish market next door had been built and operated by her grandfather. Her uncle had been a lobsterman. All in the family!

Roberta has always been involved in the arts and earned a Bachelor's degree in Voice Performance. After graduation and while waiting for the Metropolitan Opera to call(!), she enjoyed her performance career and helped organize the North Kingstown Community Chorus. She was their Director for many years. Roberta is also a member of the North Kingstown Arts Council and owner of S.P.INK Designs, a cross stitch design company.

Having five grandchildren and five great-grandchildren, it led her to think about her time spent growing up in a small town, and she decided to share her memories. Along came Nicholas the Cat who showed her the way to tell his stories and adventures along with Roberta's! Thanks Nicholas!

ABOUT THE ILLUSTRATOR

Jeff has always felt a deep love and interest in the arts, and throughout his life has participated in a variety of artistic endeavors. Starting as a young boy, he has been guided by his strong interest in art and his curiosity for the natural world. As a child he could often be found drawing, painting, or making small clay sculptures of people and animals. One of his childhood dreams was to someday live by the sea.

Jeff worked as a mental health professional for thirty-four years helping many people to cope with some of life's diverse challenges. In retirement, Jeff reconnected with his artistic and creative interests. He then met 'Nicholas the Cat' through his longtime friend, singing coach, and choral director, Roberta Belanger. Roberta and Jeff collaborated closely for several years to come up with a distinctive look for the books' illustrations. Their goal was to create images of Nicholas and his friends that would convey the timeless yet current feeling of the stories, and that would delight readers of any age. It was Roberta's influence that inspired and challenged Jeff to paint and draw again after many years, and to refine his artistic techniques.

Some of Jeff's diverse interests have included volunteering at various cultural and performing arts centers. He enjoys boating, hiking, skiing, and has a passion for cooking, gardening, and studying architecture and design. He frequently takes on home renovation projects, and likes to travel and learn about different cultures, and about the natural world. He is a fan of classic movies, and revels in singing baritone with a community chorus. He also enjoys spending time with family and friends, and practices yoga and meditation. Jeff resides with his family and two cats, and has realized his childhood dream of living near the sea in a small coastal town in Rhode Island.

ACKNOWLEDGMENTS

Welcome to the third book in the **Nicholas the Cat** series. This book is based on many childhood memories shared with my brother Tom, and my sister Linda.

Linda helped with editing and story lines from book one. We, of course, shared the same memories and were delighted to make Nicholas the Cat the storyteller in these books. Growing up, my Dad was a commercial fisherman on the 'real' big fishing dock. As kids, we spent many days swimming in the bay in Wickford, RI!

Barbara Findley has been an editor since book I, also. She is very knowledgeable of children's books having raised three boys. She was extremely insightful in the direction of the stories and grammar. Excellent editor.

Linda Epich and Dana Poulin joined the editing team for book three. It is amazing to me that after three people have read and edited all the chapters, these two ladies could still find errors and make suggestions from possessives (ugh), to tenses. Thank you!

My husband Bob listened to me reading the chapters out loud in my office and often wondered who I was talking to. I interrupted his work constantly with questions and to get opinions. He never complained.

FOODS YOU CAN SHARE WITH YOUR PET

These foods are safe to share with pets when unseasoned, cut into pieces and given sparingly in small portions! Be sure to remove any seeds, cores, stems or peels from the fruits. Meat should be lean, cooked, and free of bones.

Apples	Bananas	Beef
Blueberries	Broccoli	Cantaloupe
Carrots	Cauliflower	Celery
Cheese	Chicken	Cooked Pumpkin
Green Beans	Kiwi	Pineapple
Popcorn	Pork	Strawberries
Turkey	X-ylitol-free Peanut Butter	

11 COMMON PLANTS THAT ARE SAFE FOR CATS AND DOGS

American Rubber Plant	Parlor Palm
Cast Iron Plant	African Violet
Phalaenopsis Orchid	Boston Fern
Spider Plant	Christmas Cactus
Donkey's Tail	Blue Echiveria
Gerbera Daisy	

ASPCA – ANIMAL POISON CONTROL CENTER
888-426-4435

CPSIA information can be obtained
at www.ICGtesting.com
Printed in the USA
JSHW021017161222
34938JS00001B/39